Table Of Contents

Chapter 1: Introduction to Building a Private Counselling Practice

Why Do You Want to be in Private Practice?

For many trainee counsellors, the idea of running a private practice is an enticing prospect. The notion of having full control over your schedule, choosing your clients, and creating your own therapeutic approach can be incredibly appealing. However, before embarking on this journey, it is important to reflect on your motivations and ask yourself, "Why do I want to be in private practice?"

One of the primary reasons trainee counsellors aspire to run their own private practice is the desire for autonomy. Working in a private practice allows you to set your own hours, choose your clients, and determine the direction of your therapeutic work. This level of independence can be empowering and fulfilling, as it allows you to tailor your practice to your specific interests and values.

Another motivation for entering private practice is the potential for financial stability and success. By running your own practice, you have the opportunity to set your own fees and determine your income. While this can be a significant advantage, it is important to remember that building a successful private practice requires time, effort, and marketing skills. It is crucial to develop a solid business plan and have a realistic understanding of the financial aspects of running a practice.

Furthermore, being in private practice offers the opportunity to create a unique therapeutic space that aligns with your personal vision and values. As a trainee counsellor, you may have already developed a specific therapeutic approach or a niche area of expertise. Running a private practice allows you to fully embody and express these professional qualities, attracting clients who resonate with your unique offering.

Lastly, being in private practice provides a sense of professional fulfillment and personal growth. As the owner of your practice, you have the autonomy to continuously learn, develop, and refine your skills. You have the freedom to pursue additional trainings, attend conferences, and stay up-to-date with the latest advancements in the field. This ongoing professional development not only benefits your clients but also enhances your own self-confidence and satisfaction as a therapist.

However, it is essential to acknowledge that private practice also comes with its own challenges. It requires a strong business mindset, effective marketing strategies, and the ability to navigate the administrative aspects of running a practice. It is important to carefully weigh the pros and cons before committing to this path.

In conclusion, the desire to be in private practice as a trainee counsellor can be driven by various factors such as autonomy, financial stability, the opportunity to create a unique therapeutic space, and professional fulfillment. However, it is crucial to thoroughly consider the challenges and responsibilities that come with running a private practice. By doing so, you can make an informed decision and embark on a rewarding and successful journey as an entrepreneur in the field of counselling.

Establishing Whether Private Practice is Right For You

As a trainee counsellor, you may be considering the possibility of running your own private practice. This subchapter aims to help you determine whether this path is the right fit for you and provides guidance on what to consider before embarking on this entrepreneurial journey.

Running a private counselling practice can be an incredibly rewarding experience, allowing you to have more control over your work and create a practice tailored to your unique approach and values. However, it is crucial to assess your readiness and suitability for this venture before taking the leap. Here are some key factors to consider:

1. Self-reflection: Begin by examining your motivations and aspirations for starting a private practice. Are you driven by a desire for autonomy and independence? Do you have a passion for helping others and a strong belief in the potential of private practice? Reflecting on these questions will help you gauge your commitment and determine if the challenges associated with running a business align with your personal and professional goals.

2. Financial considerations: Establishing a private practice requires financial investments, such as office space, marketing, and ongoing professional development. Evaluate your financial stability and assess whether you have the resources to sustain your practice during the initial stages when building a client base may take time.

3. Business acumen: Running a private practice involves more than just providing counselling services. You will need to develop business skills, including marketing, networking, and financial management. Assess your willingness to learn and acquire these skills or consider partnering with someone who can complement your strengths.

4. Time management: Running a private practice demands effective time management skills. Consider the time required for administrative tasks, marketing efforts, client sessions, and ongoing professional development. Reflect on your ability to balance these aspects and maintain your own well-being.

5. Ethical considerations: Private practice comes with ethical responsibilities, including maintaining confidentiality, managing dual relationships, and

ensuring appropriate boundaries. Evaluate your readiness to navigate these ethical challenges and commit to upholding high ethical standards.

Before committing to establishing a private practice, it is recommended to seek guidance from experienced professionals or mentors who have successfully embarked on a similar journey. They can provide insights into the challenges and rewards associated with running a private counselling practice.

Remember, establishing a private practice requires careful consideration and self-reflection. By exploring your motivations, financial readiness, business acumen, time management skills, and ethical responsibilities, you can make an informed decision about whether private practice is the right path for you.

Understanding the Transition from Trainee to Entrepreneur

Making the transition from trainee to entrepreneur can be an exciting yet challenging journey for aspiring counsellors. As you embark on this path, it is essential to equip yourself with a solid understanding of the process and the unique challenges that lie ahead. This subchapter aims to guide trainee counsellors in comprehending the intricacies involved in transitioning from a trainee to a successful entrepreneur running a private counselling practice.

The first step in this journey is to recognize the shift in mindset required. As a trainee, you were primarily focused on developing your counselling skills and gaining experience. However, as an entrepreneur, you now need to shift your focus towards building and managing a business. This includes understanding the financial aspects, marketing strategies, and networking opportunities required to establish a thriving private practice.

One of the key aspects to consider during this transition is the importance of building a strong professional network. As a trainee, you likely had access to supervisors, mentors, and colleagues who provided guidance and support. However, as an entrepreneur, you will need to proactively seek out similar support networks, such as professional associations, networking events, and online communities. These connections can provide invaluable advice, collaboration opportunities, and emotional support during the early stages of your private practice.

Additionally, understanding the financial implications of running a private practice is crucial. Trainees may not have had much exposure to the financial aspects of counselling, such as setting fees, managing expenses, and handling insurance billing. It is essential to educate yourself on these topics to ensure the financial sustainability of your practice.

Furthermore, marketing your services effectively is vital for attracting clients to your private practice. As a trainee, clients may have been assigned to you, but as an entrepreneur, you must actively promote your practice and differentiate yourself from competitors. This subchapter will explore various marketing strategies, including online platforms, social media, and referrals, to help you develop a solid marketing plan.

Ultimately, the transition from trainee to entrepreneur requires a multifaceted approach. It involves a shift in mindset, building a professional network, understanding the financial aspects, and implementing effective marketing strategies. By embracing this transformation and equipping yourself with the necessary knowledge and skills, you will be well-prepared to build a successful private counselling practice.

The Importance of Experience

In the world of counselling, experience is paramount. As trainee counsellors, you may be wondering why experience is so crucial in building a successful private practice. This subchapter aims to shed light on the significance of experience and how it can benefit you as you embark on your journey to becoming an entrepreneur in the counselling field.

First and foremost, experience allows you to develop and refine your skills. While theoretical knowledge is essential, it is through hands-on experience that you truly learn and grow as a counsellor. Every client you encounter presents a unique set of challenges and circumstances, and it is through these interactions that you learn how to adapt your approach, build rapport, and effectively address their needs. The more experience you gain, the more confident and competent you become in handling a wide range of client cases.

Furthermore, experience provides you with invaluable insight and wisdom. As you work with clients over time, you begin to notice patterns, recurring themes, and common struggles. This knowledge enables you to anticipate certain challenges and tailor your interventions accordingly. Additionally, experience helps you develop a deep understanding of human behavior, emotions, and the complexities of the human mind. This understanding allows you to offer more insightful and impactful guidance to your clients.

In addition to enhancing your skills and knowledge, experience also builds your reputation and credibility. Clients seek counsellors who have a proven track record of success and who are experienced in dealing with their specific issues. By accumulating experience, you demonstrate to potential clients that you have the expertise and competence to guide them through their challenges. This, in turn, helps you attract and retain clients, which is crucial for building a thriving private practice.

Lastly, experience allows you to establish a network of professional connections. As you work with different clients, you may collaborate with other professionals in the field, such as psychologists, psychiatrists, or social workers. These connections can be invaluable in terms of referrals, consultation, and ongoing professional development. By actively seeking out opportunities to gain experience and connect with other professionals, you can expand your network and open doors to further growth and success.

In conclusion, experience is the foundation upon which a successful private counselling practice is built. It provides you with the skills, insight, reputation, and connections necessary to thrive in your entrepreneurial journey. Embrace every opportunity to gain experience, learn from each client interaction, and continuously seek ways to further develop and refine your expertise. Remember, the more experience you accumulate, the more confident and successful you will become as a private practice counsellor.

Running Your Own Practice is Hard Work

Starting your own private counselling practice can be an exciting and rewarding experience, but it is important to acknowledge that it is also hard work. As a trainee counsellor, taking the leap from being a trainee to becoming an entrepreneur can bring about a multitude of challenges that you may not have anticipated. However, with the right mindset and preparation, you can overcome these obstacles and build a successful private counselling practice.

One of the first challenges you may encounter is establishing a client base. As a trainee counsellor, you may have had the luxury of being assigned clients or having a steady flow of referrals. However, when you start your own practice, attracting clients becomes your responsibility. This means marketing yourself effectively, networking with other professionals, and utilizing various promotional strategies. It can be intimidating at first, but with persistence and a strong referral network, you can build a solid client base over time.

Another challenge you may face is managing the administrative side of running a practice. From scheduling appointments and keeping client records to handling billing and insurance claims, there are numerous administrative tasks that require your attention. As a counsellor, your focus is on helping clients, but running a practice also demands attention to the business side of things. It is crucial to develop efficient systems and processes to ensure that administrative tasks do not become overwhelming and detract from your counselling work.

Maintaining a healthy work-life balance is another aspect that requires your attention. When you are the sole proprietor of your practice, it can be tempting to work long hours and neglect self-care. However, it is essential to establish boundaries and prioritize your well-being. Setting clear working hours, taking breaks, and engaging in self-care activities are all essential practices to prevent burnout and maintain your overall mental and physical health.

Lastly, financial management is a significant aspect of running your own practice. As an entrepreneur, you need to be knowledgeable about budgeting, bookkeeping, and tax obligations. It is crucial to keep track of your expenses, establish a fee structure that aligns with your market, and ensure that your practice remains financially sustainable.

Running your own private counselling practice is undoubtedly hard work, but it is also highly rewarding. By being prepared for the challenges that may arise, you can navigate the journey from trainee to entrepreneur successfully. With dedication, perseverance, and a commitment to providing quality counselling services, you can build a thriving private practice that fulfills both your professional and personal goals.

Chapter 2: Establishing a Strong Foundation

Membership and Accreditation

Becoming a member of a professional counseling organization and obtaining accreditation is a crucial step for trainee counselors who aspire to run a successful private practice. Membership and accreditation not only provide credibility and recognition but also offer numerous benefits and resources that can enhance your professional development and help you establish yourself in the field.

One of the most significant advantages of membership in a professional counseling organization is the access to a supportive community. Being part of a network of like-minded professionals can offer you guidance, mentorship opportunities, and a platform to exchange ideas and experiences. By joining a counseling organization, you can connect with seasoned practitioners who have already navigated the challenges of running a private practice and gain valuable insights from their expertise.

Additionally, becoming a member allows you to stay up-to-date with the latest trends and advancements in the counseling field. Professional organizations often offer continuing education programs, workshops, and conferences that can deepen your knowledge and sharpen your skills. These events also provide an excellent opportunity to network with other professionals, potential clients, and referral sources.

Accreditation is another essential aspect of building a private counseling practice. Accreditation demonstrates to potential clients and stakeholders that you meet the highest professional standards and adhere to a code of ethics. It assures clients that you have the necessary training, skills, and competencies to provide quality counseling services.

While each professional counseling organization has its own accreditation process, common requirements may include a certain number of supervised counseling hours, completion of specific training programs, and passing an examination. Achieving accreditation can be a rigorous process, but the benefits outweigh the challenges. Accreditation enhances your professional credibility and can significantly increase your chances of attracting clients and referrals.

Moreover, being a member of an accredited organization may make you eligible for insurance reimbursements, which can expand your client base and increase your revenue. Many insurance providers require that counselors be affiliated with an accredited professional organization to qualify for reimbursement.

In conclusion, membership in a professional counseling organization and obtaining accreditation play a vital role in the journey from trainee to successful private practice owner. The benefits of membership, including access to a supportive community, professional development opportunities, and networking prospects, can greatly contribute to your growth as a counselor. Accreditation, on the other hand, ensures that you are recognized as a qualified and ethical practitioner, which can attract clients and open doors to reimbursement opportunities. By prioritizing membership and accreditation, you are laying a solid foundation for your private counseling practice and positioning yourself for long-term success.

Defining Your Mission and Vision

As a trainee counsellor embarking on the journey of building a private counselling practice, it is essential to start by defining your mission and vision. This subchapter will guide you through the process of identifying and articulating your purpose, values, and long-term goals. Developing a clear mission and vision statement will not only give you a sense of direction but also help you establish a strong foundation for your practice.

Mission Statement: Your mission statement is a concise declaration of your practice's purpose and the primary reason for its existence. It should reflect your passion, the needs you aim to address, and the impact you aspire to make on your clients. Creating a mission statement will require you to reflect on your values, strengths, and the unique qualities you bring to your counselling practice. It should be inspiring, authentic, and align with your professional goals.

Vision Statement: Your vision statement represents the desired future state of your practice. It paints a vivid picture of what you aspire to achieve in the long run. Crafting a compelling vision statement involves envisioning the impact you want to have on your clients' lives, the community, and the counselling profession as a whole. It should be aspirational, yet attainable, and serve as a source of motivation throughout your entrepreneurial journey.

Articulating Values: Determine the core values that will guide your practice's operations and decision-making process. Values such as empathy, compassion, integrity, and professionalism are often essential in the counselling field. Understanding your values will help you establish a strong ethical framework and ensure that your practice is aligned with your personal and professional beliefs.

Long-Term Goals: Setting long-term goals is crucial for your practice's growth and sustainability. These goals should be specific, measurable, achievable, relevant, and time-bound (SMART). Consider the number of clients you aim to serve, the services you want to offer, and the professional development opportunities you seek to pursue. Your long-term goals will evolve over time, but having a clear direction will help you stay focused and motivated.

By defining your mission and vision, you lay the groundwork for a successful private counselling practice. These statements will guide your decision-making, attract your ideal clients, and differentiate you from competitors. Take the time to reflect on your purpose and aspirations, and don't be afraid to revise and refine your mission and vision as your practice grows. Embrace the journey from trainee to entrepreneur and build a counselling practice that truly reflects who you are and the impact you want to make in the lives of others.

Setting Goals for Your Practice

As a trainee counsellor, the idea of running your own private practice may seem daunting. However, with careful planning and goal setting, you can turn your dream into a reality. This subchapter will guide you through the process of setting goals for your practice, helping you create a roadmap for success.

The first step in setting goals for your practice is to define your vision. What is your ultimate goal as a counsellor? Do you want to specialize in a particular niche, such as working with children or couples? Understanding your long-term vision will help you set meaningful goals that align with your values and aspirations.

Once you have a clear vision, it's time to set specific, measurable, achievable, relevant, and time-bound (SMART) goals. Start by identifying what you hope to achieve in the next year, such as obtaining a certain number of clients or completing additional training in a specific therapeutic approach. Break these goals down into smaller, actionable steps that you can take on a daily, weekly, or monthly basis.

Goal setting is not just about the end result; it's also about the journey. Along the way, be sure to celebrate your accomplishments and track your progress. This will help you stay motivated and focused on your goals, even when challenges arise.

In addition to short-term goals, it's essential to set long-term goals for your practice. Where do you see yourself in five or ten years? Do you want to expand your practice, hire additional therapists, or open multiple locations? By envisioning your future, you can create a roadmap that will guide you towards your ultimate vision.

Remember that goal setting is a dynamic process. As you gain experience and your practice evolves, your goals may change. Regularly review and revise your goals to ensure they remain relevant and aligned with your evolving needs and aspirations.

In conclusion, setting goals for your private counselling practice is crucial for your success as a trainee counsellor turned entrepreneur. By defining your vision, setting SMART goals, tracking your progress, and regularly reviewing and revising your goals, you can create a roadmap that will guide you towards building a thriving private practice. With determination and perseverance, you can turn your dream into a reality and make a meaningful impact in the lives of your clients.

Identifying Your Target Market

As a trainee counsellor on the path to building your private practice, one of the most crucial steps is identifying your target market. This subchapter will guide you through the process of understanding your ideal clients and how to effectively reach them.

Your target market is the specific group of people who are most likely to benefit from your counselling services. By defining your target market, you can tailor your marketing efforts and services to meet their unique needs. This strategic approach will not only attract more clients but also allow you to provide the best possible care.

To begin, take some time to reflect on your own interests, experiences, and strengths as a counsellor. What types of issues are you most passionate about addressing? Are there specific populations or age groups that you feel particularly drawn to working with? By considering these factors, you can start to narrow down your target market.

Next, conduct market research to gain insights into the needs and preferences of your potential clients. Look into existing research, surveys, and data related to the counselling field. This information will help you understand the current demand for counselling services in different niches and identify any gaps in the market that you could potentially fill.

Additionally, consider conducting focus groups or interviews with individuals who may fit within your target market. This will allow you to gather firsthand feedback and gain a deeper understanding of their specific needs and preferences. By listening to their stories and challenges, you can tailor your services to better address their unique circumstances.

Once you have identified your target market, it's important to develop a compelling marketing strategy to effectively reach and engage potential clients. This may include creating a professional website, utilizing social media platforms, and networking within relevant professional communities. By utilizing these marketing techniques, you can ensure that your counselling practice becomes visible to the right people.

Remember, identifying your target market is an ongoing process. As you gain more experience and receive feedback from clients, you may need to adjust your target market to better align with your skills and interests. By consistently evaluating and refining your target market, you can build a successful private counselling practice that truly meets the needs of your ideal clients.

Developing a Unique Selling Proposition

In the competitive world of counseling, it is crucial for trainee counselors to stand out from the crowd and establish a successful private practice. A unique selling proposition (USP) is a key component in achieving this. A USP differentiates you from fellow practitioners and helps potential clients understand why they should choose you as their counselor. In this subchapter, we will explore the importance of developing a strong USP and provide practical tips on how to create one.

To begin, understanding your niche is essential. As a trainee counselor, you should identify the specific area or population you want to serve. Whether it's couples therapy, addiction counseling, or working with adolescents, narrowing down your focus allows you to develop expertise and tailor your USP accordingly. By catering to a specific niche, you can address the unique needs and challenges of these clients, setting yourself apart from generalist counselors.

Next, consider your personal strengths and passions. Reflect on what sets you apart from other trainee counselors. Do you have a particular approach or therapeutic modality that resonates with you? Are you passionate about incorporating mindfulness or art therapy into your practice? These unique qualities can become the foundation of your USP and attract clients who resonate with your approach.

Additionally, conducting market research is crucial in developing a strong USP. Investigate the local counseling landscape to identify gaps or underserved areas. Are there specific populations or issues that are in high demand but lack sufficient counselors? By identifying these gaps, you can position yourself as an expert in an untapped market, making your USP even more compelling.

Crafting a compelling USP involves clearly communicating the benefits and outcomes clients can expect from working with you. Consider what value you bring to your clients and how you can articulate this in a concise and impactful manner. Are you known for creating a safe and non-judgmental space? Do you have a track record of helping clients achieve long-lasting transformation? Highlight these aspects in your USP to attract potential clients who are seeking these specific outcomes.

Finally, test and refine your USP. Share it with trusted colleagues, mentors, or even potential clients, and gather feedback. Continuously assess its effectiveness and make adjustments as needed. Remember, a USP is not set in stone, and as you grow and evolve as a counselor, it may require updates to reflect your changing expertise and interests.

Developing a unique selling proposition is a vital step for trainee counselors looking to establish a private practice. By identifying your niche, leveraging your strengths, conducting market research, and effectively communicating the value you bring to clients, you can create a compelling USP that sets you apart and attracts your ideal clients.

Chapter 3: Creating a Business Plan

Understanding the Purpose of a Business Plan

As a trainee counsellor, you may be wondering why you need a business plan for your private counselling practice. After all, your focus is on helping individuals and making a positive impact, right? While that is undoubtedly important, having a well-thought-out business plan is essential for the success and sustainability of your practice. In this subchapter, we will explore the purpose of a business plan and its significance in building and running your private counselling practice.

First and foremost, a business plan serves as a roadmap for your practice. It outlines your goals, objectives, and strategies for achieving them. By clearly defining your vision and mission, you can create a solid foundation upon which to build your practice. A business plan allows you to establish a direction and set realistic and achievable targets, helping you stay focused and motivated.

Additionally, a well-crafted business plan helps you understand the market and competition within your niche. Conducting market research allows you to identify your target audience, their needs, and the current demand for counselling services. This knowledge enables you to tailor your services to meet the unique requirements of your clients, giving you a competitive edge. Understanding your competition also allows you to differentiate yourself by offering specialized services or implementing innovative methods.

Furthermore, a business plan is a crucial tool for securing financial support. Whether you are seeking loans from a bank or investment from external sources, a comprehensive and professional business plan will demonstrate your dedication, competence, and potential for success. It showcases your financial projections, budgeting, and marketing strategies, providing potential investors or lenders with a clear understanding of your practice's viability and profitability.

Lastly, a business plan enables you to evaluate and monitor your progress. By setting measurable goals and key performance indicators (KPIs), you can assess your practice's growth and make necessary adjustments along the way. Regularly reviewing and updating your business plan ensures that you remain adaptable to changes in the market and industry trends, allowing you to stay ahead of the curve.

In conclusion, understanding the purpose of a business plan is paramount for any trainee counsellor looking to establish a successful private practice. It serves as a guiding tool, helping you define your vision, understand your target market, obtain financial support, and monitor your progress. By investing time and effort into crafting a comprehensive business plan, you are setting yourself up for long-term success and sustainability in your journey from trainee to entrepreneur.

Conducting Market Research

One of the most crucial steps in building a successful private counseling practice is conducting market research. As a trainee counselor looking to transition into entrepreneurship, understanding the market and your potential clients is essential for long-term success. This subchapter will guide you through the process of conducting effective market research, enabling you to make informed decisions and develop strategies that will set you apart in the counseling industry.

Market research involves gathering and analyzing data about your target market, including demographics, preferences, and needs. By understanding your potential clients, you can tailor your services to meet their specific requirements, giving you a competitive edge. Here are some key steps to conduct effective market research:

1. Identify your target market: Begin by defining the specific group of clients you want to serve. Are you targeting a particular age group, gender, or socioeconomic background? Understanding your target market will help you focus your research efforts.

2. Determine the demand: Assess the demand for counseling services in your area. Look for statistics, trends, and reports on mental health issues and the availability of counseling services. This information will give you a sense of the potential market size and the competition you may face.

3. Analyze your competition: Research other private counseling practices in your area and identify what sets them apart. Examine their pricing, services offered, and target market. Understanding your competition will help you differentiate yourself and develop a unique selling proposition.

4. Conduct surveys and interviews: Engage directly with potential clients to gather insights about their counseling needs, preferences, and experiences. Surveys and interviews can provide valuable feedback and help you refine your services to meet client expectations.

5. Utilize online resources: Take advantage of online platforms, such as social media, forums, and counseling directories, to gather information about potential clients and engage with them directly. These platforms can also be used to promote your services and build a strong online presence.

Remember, market research is an ongoing process. As your counseling practice evolves, it is important to continue monitoring the market and adapting your strategies accordingly. By conducting thorough market research, you will be equipped with the knowledge to make informed decisions, effectively position your practice, and attract the right clients.

Assessing Your Competitors

In the competitive world of running a private counselling practice, it is crucial for trainee counsellors to assess their competitors before venturing into the market. Understanding the landscape and being aware of your rivals can provide valuable insights and help you position your practice effectively. This subchapter will guide you through the process of assessing your competitors, enabling you to make informed decisions and stand out in the field.

Firstly, identify your direct competitors – those who offer similar counselling services in your area. Look for private practices that target the same client base as you. Research their services, pricing, and marketing strategies. Assess the strengths and weaknesses of each competitor, noting what makes them successful or where they may be lacking.

Next, analyze their online presence. Explore their websites, social media profiles, and online reviews. Pay attention to the overall user experience, the quality of their content, and how they engage with their audience. This evaluation will give you an idea of their brand image and the strategies they use to attract clients.

Furthermore, consider the unique selling points (USPs) of your competitors. What sets them apart? Are they known for their specialization in a particular area? Do they offer additional services or innovative approaches? Understanding their USPs will help you identify gaps in the market and find ways to differentiate your practice.

Don't forget to study your indirect competitors as well. These may include community centers, hospitals, or online counselling platforms. Assess their strengths and weaknesses, as they may offer alternative solutions to your potential clients. Understanding the advantages they have over private practices can help you refine your marketing strategies.

Additionally, networking with other professionals in the field can provide valuable insights. Attend conferences, workshops, or join online communities to connect with experienced counsellors. Engaging in conversations with them will not only expand your knowledge but also offer insights into their perceptions of the industry and competitors.

Lastly, use the information gathered through your assessment to refine your own practice's positioning and marketing strategies. Identify the gaps in the market and tailor your services to meet the needs of your target audience.

Highlight your unique strengths and communicate them effectively through your branding and marketing materials.

Assessing your competitors is an ongoing process. As you establish your practice, keep an eye on the changing landscape and adjust your strategies accordingly. By staying informed and adapting to the market, you can position yourself as a reputable and sought-after counsellor in your niche.

Defining Your Services and Pricing

As a trainee counsellor, the idea of running a private practice may seem daunting. However, with careful planning and a clear understanding of your services and pricing, you can successfully build a thriving counseling practice that meets the needs of your clients and supports your professional growth.

Defining your services is a crucial step in establishing your private practice. Consider the populations you wish to work with and the specific issues you want to address. Are you interested in working with individuals, couples, or families? Do you have expertise in a particular area such as trauma, addiction, or relationship counseling? Defining your niche will not only help you attract the right clients but also enhance your credibility and expertise.

Once you have identified your target population and specialization, it is important to determine the scope of your services. Will you offer short-term or long-term counseling? Do you plan to provide individual or group therapy? Consider the number of sessions you are willing to offer and the duration of each session. Defining these parameters will not only help you manage your time effectively but also ensure that your clients understand what to expect.

Pricing your services is another crucial aspect of running a private practice. It is important to strike a balance between setting a fair fee for your expertise and ensuring that your services remain accessible to potential clients. Conduct market research to determine the average fees charged by other counselors in your area. Consider factors such as your level of experience, specialization, and the local demand for counseling services when determining your fees.

Additionally, consider offering different payment options to accommodate diverse client needs. Some clients may prefer paying per session, while others may benefit from package deals or sliding scale fees based on their income. Offering flexibility in pricing can help attract a wider range of clients and ensure that your services are accessible to those who may not have the means to pay the full fee.

In conclusion, defining your services and pricing is a crucial step in building a successful private counseling practice as a trainee counselor. By identifying your target population, specialization, and scope of services, you can attract the right clients and enhance your credibility. Additionally, setting fair fees and offering flexible payment options will ensure that your services remain accessible to a diverse range of clients. With careful planning and a clear understanding of your services and pricing, you can confidently embark on the journey of running your own private counseling practice.

Developing a Marketing Strategy

In order to successfully build a private counseling practice as a trainee counselor, it is crucial to develop an effective marketing strategy. While counseling skills and knowledge are undoubtedly important, without the ability to attract and retain clients, your practice may struggle to thrive. This subchapter will guide you through the process of developing a marketing strategy that will help you establish a strong and reputable presence in the counseling field.

1. Identifying Your Target Market: The first step in developing a marketing strategy is to identify your target market. Consider the specific niche or population you wish to serve, such as couples, adolescents, or individuals struggling with addiction. Understanding your target market will allow you to tailor your marketing efforts to reach and resonate with them effectively.

2. Creating a Brand Identity: Developing a strong brand identity is essential for setting yourself apart from competitors. Your brand should reflect your values, expertise, and unique selling points. Consider creating a compelling logo, designing a professional website, and developing consistent branding elements that can be applied across all marketing materials.

3. Building an Online Presence: In today's digital age, having a strong online presence is vital for attracting clients. Create a user-friendly website that showcases your services, expertise, and testimonials from previous clients. Utilize social media platforms to engage with your target audience, share valuable content, and establish yourself as an authority in your field.

4. Networking and Collaboration: Building relationships within the counseling community and related industries is an effective way to expand your reach. Attend conferences, workshops, and networking events to connect with other professionals, exchange ideas, and potentially collaborate on projects. Join professional associations and consider offering workshops or training programs to establish yourself as a trusted expert.

5. Implementing Effective Marketing Techniques: Utilize a variety of marketing techniques to reach your target audience. Consider traditional methods such as print advertisements, brochures, and business cards. Additionally, explore digital marketing strategies like search engine optimization (SEO), content marketing, and online advertising to increase your visibility and attract potential clients.

6. Tracking and Evaluating Results: As you implement your marketing strategy, it is essential to track and evaluate the results of your efforts. Monitor the effectiveness of different marketing channels, analyze website traffic, and track client inquiries. By regularly evaluating the success of your marketing initiatives, you can make data-driven decisions and refine your strategy accordingly.

By developing and implementing a well-rounded marketing strategy, you can effectively promote your private counseling practice to your target audience. Remember, building a successful practice takes time and effort, but with a solid marketing foundation, you will be well-equipped to navigate the journey from trainee to entrepreneur.

Chapter 4: Legal and Ethical Considerations

Registering Your Business (UK)

As a trainee counsellor embarking on the journey of building your private practice, the process of registering your business is an important step to ensure legal compliance and establish a solid foundation for your venture. In the United Kingdom, there are certain requirements and procedures that you need to be aware of when it comes to registering your business. This subchapter will guide you through the essential steps of registering your counselling practice in the UK.

The first step in registering your business is choosing a legal structure. As a sole practitioner, you may opt for a sole trader status, which is the simplest and most common form of business ownership. Alternatively, you can consider setting up a limited company or a partnership, depending on your individual circumstances and preferences.

Once you have decided on the legal structure, the next step is to register your business with the appropriate authorities. In the UK, this involves registering with Her Majesty's Revenue and Customs (HMRC) for tax purposes. You will need to obtain a Unique Taxpayer Reference (UTR) number and register for self-assessment as a sole trader. If you choose to set up a limited company, you will need to register with Companies House.

Additionally, it is important to consider whether you need to register with professional bodies or organizations relevant to your counselling practice. For example, if you plan to work with children or vulnerable adults, you may need to register with the Disclosure and Barring Service (DBS) and obtain an Enhanced DBS Certificate. Similarly, if you specialize in a particular therapeutic approach, you might want to consider joining professional associations such as the British Association for Counselling and

Psychotherapy (BACP) or the United Kingdom Council for Psychotherapy (UKCP).

Furthermore, don't forget to check whether you need any licenses or permits to operate your counselling practice. Depending on your location and the nature of your services, you may need to obtain local council permits or comply with specific regulations. It's crucial to research and understand the requirements in your area to ensure full compliance.

Registering your business is a crucial step towards establishing a solid foundation for your private counselling practice. By following the necessary processes and meeting legal obligations, you can ensure that your business operates smoothly and ethically. Take the time to research and understand the specific requirements for your location and niche, as compliance with regulations will contribute to your credibility and professionalism as a trainee counsellor running a private practice in the UK.

Understanding Legal Requirements and Regulations (UK)

As a trainee counsellor, embarking on the journey of building your private counselling practice can be both exciting and overwhelming. While the prospect of being your own boss and helping clients on your terms is undoubtedly appealing, it is crucial to understand the legal requirements and regulations that govern the practice of counselling in the UK.

Licensing and Registration: In the United Kingdom, counsellors are not legally required to obtain a license to practice. However, it is highly recommended to join a professional body such as the British Association for Counselling and Psychotherapy (BACP) or the United Kingdom Council for Psychotherapy (UKCP). Membership in such organizations ensures that you adhere to their ethical guidelines and guarantees a level of professional credibility.

Confidentiality and Data Protection: Maintaining client confidentiality is of utmost importance in the counselling profession. Familiarize yourself with the legal obligations surrounding client confidentiality, including the Data Protection Act 2018 and the General Data Protection Regulation (GDPR). Ensure that you have robust systems in place to securely store and handle client data.

Insurance: Obtaining professional indemnity insurance is essential for protecting yourself, your clients, and your practice against any potential claims. Insurance provides reassurance and peace of mind, safeguarding you in case of unforeseen circumstances or complaints.

Safeguarding Vulnerable Clients: It is crucial to have a comprehensive understanding of safeguarding protocols and procedures, particularly when working with vulnerable clients such as children or individuals with mental health issues. Familiarize yourself with local safeguarding boards and organizations that provide guidance on safeguarding practices.

Advertising and Marketing: When promoting your private counselling practice, be aware of the Advertising Standards Authority (ASA) regulations. Ensure that your marketing materials, including your website and social media content, are accurate, ethical, and do not make false claims about your services or qualifications.

Professional Development: Continuing professional development (CPD) is vital for trainee counsellors to stay up-to-date with the evolving legal and ethical landscape. Engage in regular CPD activities, such as attending workshops, conferences, and training courses, to enhance your skills and knowledge.

By understanding and adhering to the legal requirements and regulations that govern the counselling profession in the UK, you can establish a strong foundation for your private practice. Compliance with these regulations not only ensures the safety and well-being of your clients but also contributes to your professional credibility and success as a trainee counsellor turned entrepreneur.

Maintaining Confidentiality and Privacy

Confidentiality and privacy are fundamental aspects of running a successful private counselling practice. As a trainee counsellor, it is crucial to understand the importance of establishing and maintaining a safe and secure environment for your clients. In this subchapter, we will explore the key principles and practices that will help you uphold confidentiality and privacy in your counselling practice.

First and foremost, it is essential to establish a clear understanding of confidentiality with your clients from the very beginning. During the initial sessions, take the time to explain the limits of confidentiality and the circumstances under which you may need to breach it. This will help to build trust and ensure that your clients feel comfortable sharing their deepest concerns with you.

In addition to verbal explanations, it is advisable to provide a written confidentiality agreement or policy for your clients to sign. This document should outline the measures you have in place to protect their privacy and the exceptions to confidentiality, such as when there is a risk of harm to oneself or others. By obtaining their informed consent, you demonstrate your commitment to maintaining confidentiality while also protecting yourself legally.

To further safeguard client information, it is crucial to implement robust security measures. This includes keeping all client records and session notes securely stored and protected from unauthorized access. Consider investing in a secure electronic health record system or encrypted software to ensure the highest level of privacy for your clients.

Moreover, it is important to establish boundaries around client communication. Clearly define the acceptable modes of communication, such as phone calls or emails, and establish guidelines for when and how you will respond. Encourage clients to use secure channels when discussing sensitive or personal matters, such as encrypted email or secure video conferencing platforms.

Lastly, as a trainee counsellor, it is important to seek ongoing supervision and consultation to ensure that you are maintaining confidentiality and privacy effectively. Regularly discussing cases with a supervisor or a peer support group can help you navigate any ethical dilemmas and ensure that you are adhering to the highest standards of professional conduct.

By prioritizing confidentiality and privacy in your counselling practice, you will not only demonstrate your dedication to ethical standards but also foster a safe and trusting environment for your clients. Upholding these principles is not only an ethical obligation but also essential for the success and growth of your private counselling practice.

Ensuring Ethical Practices in Counselling

As trainee counsellors embark on their journey towards building a private counselling practice, it is crucial to understand and prioritize the importance of ethical practices. Ethical considerations play a vital role in establishing a reputable and successful counselling business. This subchapter aims to provide trainee counsellors with insights and guidelines on how to ensure ethical practices in their counselling careers.

First and foremost, it is essential to familiarize oneself with the ethical guidelines and codes of conduct specific to the field of counselling. These codes, often established by professional counseling organizations, serve as a framework for ethical practices. Trainee counsellors should thoroughly study these guidelines and ensure that their practice aligns with the principles outlined within.

Confidentiality is a cornerstone of ethical counselling practices. It is imperative to create a safe and secure environment for clients where they feel comfortable sharing their thoughts and emotions. Trainee counsellors must maintain strict confidentiality and inform clients of the limitations to this confidentiality, such as the need to disclose information if there is a risk of harm to the client or others.

Informed consent is another crucial aspect of ethical counselling. Trainee counsellors must provide clients with comprehensive information about the counselling process, including the purpose, duration, and potential risks or benefits. Clients should have a clear understanding of what to expect and have the autonomy to make informed decisions about their treatment.

Boundaries and dual relationships should be carefully managed to avoid conflicts of interest or potential harm to clients. Trainee counsellors must establish and maintain appropriate professional boundaries, refraining from engaging in personal relationships with clients. Additionally, they should ensure that their personal beliefs and values do not interfere with the client's therapeutic process.

Continuing professional development is vital for trainee counsellors to stay updated with the latest ethical practices and trends in the field. Engaging in regular supervision, attending workshops, and participating in ongoing training programs will enhance ethical decision-making skills and ensure the provision of high-quality counselling services.

Lastly, maintaining accurate and secure records is essential for ethical practices in counselling. Trainee counsellors should establish a systematic and confidential record-keeping process that adheres to legal and ethical requirements.

By prioritizing ethical practices, trainee counsellors can lay a solid foundation for their private counselling practice. Upholding confidentiality, informed consent, and professional boundaries, while continuously updating their knowledge through professional development, will help in building a successful and ethical counselling business.

Chapter 5: Setting Up Your Practice

Choosing a Location

One of the most critical decisions trainee counsellors face when starting their private practice is selecting the right location. The location of your counselling practice can significantly impact your success and the type of clients you attract. In this chapter, we will explore key factors to consider when choosing a location for your private counselling practice.

Firstly, it is essential to assess the demographics and needs of your target audience. Consider the population density, age groups, and socioeconomic background of the area. For instance, if you specialize in working with adolescents, it may be wise to choose a location near schools or universities. Understanding your target market will help ensure that your practice is easily accessible and relevant to potential clients.

Accessibility is another crucial factor to consider. Is the location easily reached by public transportation? Are there parking facilities available for clients who prefer to drive? Accessibility is not only important for your clients but also for you as a practitioner. You want a location that is convenient for you to commute to and from, allowing you to focus on your clients' needs rather than spending excessive time on travel.

The competition in the area is another aspect to evaluate. Are there already established counselling practices in the vicinity? While some competition can be healthy, a saturated market may make it difficult for your practice to stand out. On the other hand, if there are no counselling services nearby, it could indicate a lack of demand for your services or a potential untapped market.

Consider the infrastructure and amenities available in the location. Does the area have the necessary facilities and resources to support your practice? Look for nearby amenities such as coffee shops, restaurants, and parking areas, which can enhance the overall experience for your clients. Additionally, consider the physical space itself. Is it conducive to counselling sessions? Does it provide a comfortable and confidential environment for your clients?

Lastly, assess the cost implications of the location. A prime location might come with a higher rental or lease price, which can impact your profitability. It is crucial to find a balance between a location that meets your needs and a cost that aligns with your budget.

Choosing the right location for your private counselling practice requires careful consideration of various factors, including demographics, accessibility, competition, infrastructure, and cost. By taking the time to evaluate these aspects, you can position your practice for success and create a space that attracts and serves your ideal clients effectively.

Designing Your Office Space

Creating a comfortable and inviting office space is essential when setting up your private counselling practice. The design and layout of your office can greatly impact the overall atmosphere and the experience for your clients. In this subchapter, we will explore some key considerations for designing your office space to ensure that it promotes a positive and therapeutic environment.

First and foremost, it is important to choose a location that is easily accessible and convenient for your clients. Ideally, your office should be situated in a quiet and professional area, away from noisy distractions. Consider the parking facilities and public transportation options available nearby, as this will impact the ease with which clients can reach your office.

Once you have selected a suitable location, it is time to think about the layout and decor of your office. Start by considering the size and dimensions of the space. Ensure that it is large enough to accommodate both you and your clients comfortably. The layout should be arranged in a way that promotes privacy and confidentiality, with enough space for seating, a desk, and any additional equipment or tools you may need.

When it comes to decor, opt for soothing and neutral colors that create a calm and relaxing atmosphere. Avoid overly bright or distracting patterns that may hinder the therapeutic process. Soft lighting and natural elements, such as plants or artwork, can also contribute to a welcoming and tranquil environment.

Furthermore, consider the functionality of your office space. Invest in comfortable seating options for your clients, ensuring that they feel at ease during their sessions. Additionally, have a designated area for storing client files and any necessary paperwork, such as consent forms or intake questionnaires.

Lastly, think about the accessibility of your office space. Ensure that it is wheelchair accessible and equipped with appropriate facilities for disabled clients. Furthermore, consider the comfort of your clients by providing amenities such as water, tissues, or even a small waiting area.

Designing your office space is an important part of creating a professional and therapeutic environment for your clients. By taking into account factors such as location, layout, decor, functionality, and accessibility, you can create a space that promotes relaxation, confidentiality, and ultimately enhances the counselling experience. Remember, a well-designed office space can contribute to the success of your private counselling practice and help you establish a positive reputation among trainee counsellors and your niche market.

Working From Home

In today's ever-evolving world, the concept of working from home has become increasingly popular and accessible. For trainee counsellors, the idea of running a private practice from the comfort of their own home can be both exciting and daunting. In this subchapter, we will explore the ins and outs of working from home, providing a comprehensive guide for trainee counsellors who aspire to build a successful private counselling practice.

One of the key advantages of working from home is the flexibility it offers. As a trainee counsellor, you have the freedom to set your own schedule, choosing when to see clients and when to take breaks. This flexibility allows you to balance your personal and professional life more efficiently, which is crucial for maintaining your own well-being while supporting others.

However, working from home also presents unique challenges. Distractions, such as household chores or family members, can interfere with your focus and productivity. It is essential to establish clear boundaries and create a designated workspace that is separate from your living area. This will help you maintain a professional atmosphere and minimize interruptions during sessions.

Furthermore, trainee counsellors must address the ethical considerations of working from home. Confidentiality and privacy are of utmost importance when dealing with clients. It is crucial to ensure that your home office provides a safe and secure environment, where clients' information is protected. This may involve implementing appropriate technology and security measures to maintain confidentiality.

Another aspect to consider when working from home is the impact on your personal life. It is important to communicate with your loved ones about the boundaries and limitations of your work. Setting clear expectations with family members or roommates will help minimize interruptions and create a supportive environment for your practice.

Lastly, trainee counsellors must be mindful of the potential isolation that may come with working from home. Building a professional network and seeking peer support is essential. Joining professional organizations, attending conferences, and engaging in online forums can provide opportunities for collaboration, learning, and social connection.

In conclusion, working from home can be a fulfilling and viable option for trainee counsellors who aspire to run a private practice. However, it requires careful planning, establishing boundaries, and maintaining professionalism. By addressing the challenges and embracing the benefits, trainee counsellors can create a successful and fulfilling private counselling practice from the comforts of their own home.

Telephone or Remote Counselling

In recent years, the field of counselling has witnessed a significant shift towards remote counselling services, particularly telephone counselling. With advancements in technology and the increasing demands of our fast-paced lives, more and more individuals are seeking convenience and flexibility in their therapy sessions. As a trainee counsellor, it is crucial to explore the benefits and considerations of offering telephone or remote counselling in your private practice.

One of the primary advantages of telephone counselling is its accessibility. It eliminates geographical barriers, allowing you to connect with clients who may otherwise be unable to attend face-to-face sessions. This opens up opportunities to serve a broader client base and make a positive impact on individuals who might not have access to counselling otherwise. Additionally, telephone counselling provides a sense of anonymity and privacy that some clients may find more comfortable, promoting a deeper level of disclosure and engagement in the therapeutic process.

However, it is essential to recognize the unique challenges that come with providing remote counselling. Without the visual cues and non-verbal communication present in face-to-face sessions, it can be more challenging to gauge a client's emotional state accurately. As a trainee counsellor, it is crucial to develop your active listening skills and adapt your therapeutic techniques to compensate for the absence of visual cues. This may involve asking more open-ended questions, actively summarizing and reflecting the client's emotions, and staying attuned to subtle changes in their voice tone or cadence.

Furthermore, it is crucial to establish clear boundaries and guidelines for remote counselling sessions. Discuss and agree upon confidentiality, emergency protocols, and any technical issues that may arise during sessions. Ensure that you have a secure and private space for conducting telephone counselling, free from interruptions or distractions. As a trainee counsellor, it is essential to seek regular supervision and consultation to address any ethical or clinical concerns specific to remote counselling.

Offering telephone or remote counselling can be a valuable addition to your private practice. It provides convenience and accessibility to clients while broadening your reach as a therapist. As a trainee counsellor, it is vital to stay informed about the evolving guidelines and best practices for remote counselling to ensure the highest standard of care for your clients. With proper training, supervision, and a commitment to ongoing professional development, telephone counselling can be an effective and rewarding modality for your private practice.

Selecting Essential Equipment and Supplies

As a trainee counselor embarking on the journey of building a private counseling practice, it is vital to carefully consider and select the essential equipment and supplies needed to ensure a successful and efficient operation. In this subchapter, we will explore the key factors to consider when selecting these crucial items.

The first step in selecting equipment and supplies is to identify your specific needs. Consider the type of counseling you intend to specialize in and the requirements it entails. For instance, if you plan to offer online counseling services, a reliable computer with a high-speed internet connection and a webcam would be essential. On the other hand, if your practice focuses on art therapy, you may need to invest in art supplies and a dedicated space for creative expression.

Next, think about the comfort and convenience of both yourself and your clients. A comfortable and ergonomic chair is imperative for extended counseling sessions, ensuring that both you and your clients can maintain focus and engagement. Additionally, you may want to invest in a small waiting area with comfortable seating to create a welcoming and relaxing atmosphere.

Maintaining client confidentiality is of utmost importance in counseling practice. Therefore, it is crucial to have a secure filing system for client records and sensitive information. Consider investing in a lockable filing cabinet or a digital storage system with robust security measures to protect your clients' privacy.

Beyond the basic equipment, you may also need various supplies to enhance the counseling experience. Items such as notepads, pens, tissues, and water bottles can contribute to a comfortable and productive counseling environment. Additionally, having a selection of resources such as books, pamphlets, and self-help materials can be valuable in supporting your clients' personal growth and providing additional insights.

Finally, when selecting equipment and supplies, cost-effectiveness should be considered. While it is essential to invest in quality items that will contribute to the success of your practice, it is equally important to maintain a reasonable budget. Research different suppliers, compare prices, and consider purchasing second-hand items when appropriate to keep costs manageable.

By carefully selecting the essential equipment and supplies for your private counseling practice, you can create a professional and welcoming environment for your clients while ensuring your own comfort and efficiency. Remember to tailor your selections to your specific counseling niche and needs, prioritize confidentiality, and maintain a balance between quality and cost-effectiveness.

Setting Up Appointment and Billing Systems

As a trainee counsellor, one of the most important aspects of running a successful private practice is ensuring efficient appointment and billing systems. In this subchapter, we will explore the key steps to set up these systems effectively to streamline your practice and provide the best possible service to your clients.

First and foremost, it is crucial to invest in a reliable appointment scheduling software. This will not only save you time and effort but also enhance the overall client experience. Look for a user-friendly platform that allows clients to easily book appointments online, while also providing you with the flexibility to manage your schedule. Additionally, make sure the software offers automated reminders and notifications to minimize missed appointments and improve client attendance rates.

When setting up your billing system, it is essential to establish clear and transparent policies from the outset. Clearly communicate your fees, cancellation policy, and any other financial arrangements to your clients. This will ensure there are no surprises or misunderstandings down the line. Consider using an invoicing software that allows you to generate professional invoices and track payments effortlessly. This will not only help you stay organized but also ensure prompt and accurate billing.

In addition to the technical aspects, it is imperative to prioritize client confidentiality and data security when setting up these systems. Choose software that is compliant with relevant privacy regulations and prioritizes data protection. Safeguarding client information is not only ethically important but also necessary to build trust and maintain a positive professional reputation.

Furthermore, consider integrating a client management system into your practice. This will allow you to keep track of client records, progress notes, and other important documentation in one centralized location. Having easy access to this information will not only improve your efficiency but also enhance the quality of care you provide.

Lastly, it is crucial to regularly review and update your appointment and billing systems to ensure their effectiveness. Solicit feedback from clients and make necessary adjustments based on their suggestions and needs. By continuously refining these systems, you will create a seamless experience for your clients and contribute to the success of your private practice.

In conclusion, setting up efficient appointment and billing systems is vital for trainee counsellors who aspire to run a private practice. By investing in the right tools, establishing clear policies, prioritizing confidentiality, and regularly reviewing and updating these systems, you will create a professional and client-centered practice that sets you up for long-term success in your counselling career.

Establishing Record-Keeping Processes

As a trainee counsellor, one of the key aspects of running a successful private practice is establishing efficient record-keeping processes. These processes not only ensure the smooth operation of your practice but also play a crucial role in maintaining client confidentiality and meeting legal and ethical obligations.

First and foremost, it is important to understand the significance of record-keeping in the counselling profession. Keeping accurate and comprehensive records allows you to track the progress of your clients, make informed treatment decisions, and provide continuity of care. Moreover, it serves as a legal document that can protect you from liability and provide evidence of the services you have provided.

To begin establishing your record-keeping processes, start by creating a client intake form. This form should gather essential information such as the client's name, contact details, medical history, and reasons for seeking counselling. Additionally, include a section for obtaining informed consent, where clients acknowledge their understanding of the counselling process and agree to the terms and conditions of therapy.

Once you have the client intake form in place, develop a system for maintaining session notes. These notes should be written after each counselling session and should include details on the topics discussed, interventions used, progress made, and any other relevant information. It is essential to maintain objectivity and professionalism in your session notes, avoiding personal opinions or judgments.

Furthermore, consider implementing a system for tracking appointments and client payments. This can be achieved through a digital calendar or appointment scheduling software, which not only helps in managing your schedule but also sends reminders to clients. Additionally, keep a record of all financial transactions, including fees received, payment methods, and any outstanding balances.

In terms of client confidentiality, it is imperative to establish secure storage for all records. Whether you choose physical files or digital storage, ensure that they are kept in a locked and confidential location. If you opt for electronic records, make sure to use password-protected systems and encrypted storage to safeguard client information.

Lastly, familiarize yourself with the legal and ethical responsibilities related to record-keeping in your jurisdiction. Be aware of the retention period required for keeping records and the regulations regarding the disclosure of client information, especially in cases of subpoenas or court orders.

In conclusion, establishing effective and efficient record-keeping processes is a fundamental aspect of running a private counselling practice. By implementing these processes, you not only ensure the smooth operation of your practice but also ensure client confidentiality, meet legal obligations, and provide quality care to your clients. Taking the time to develop these processes from the beginning will set a solid foundation for your future practice as an entrepreneur in the counselling field.

Chapter 6: Marketing and Promoting Your Practice

Building a Professional Brand

In the competitive world of private counseling practice, building a strong professional brand is essential for trainee counselors looking to establish themselves and succeed in their careers. Your brand is not just a logo or a catchy tagline; it is a reflection of who you are as a counselor and what you bring to the table. It encompasses your unique skills, values, and expertise, and it is what sets you apart from your competitors.

To build a professional brand that resonates with your target audience and attracts clients, there are several key steps you need to take. The first step is to define your niche. What specific area of counseling are you passionate about? What types of clients do you want to work with? By focusing on a specific niche, you can position yourself as an expert and tailor your services to meet the specific needs of your target audience.

Once you have identified your niche, it is important to develop a strong online presence. In today's digital age, your website and social media profiles are often the first point of contact for potential clients. Invest in a professional website that reflects your brand and showcases your expertise. Use social media platforms such as LinkedIn, Facebook, and Instagram to share valuable content, engage with your audience, and establish yourself as a thought leader in your field.

Networking is another crucial aspect of building a professional brand. Attend industry conferences, join professional associations, and connect with other counselors and influencers in your niche. Building relationships with colleagues and mentors not only provides valuable support and guidance but also opens doors to potential referrals and collaborations.

Your brand should also be evident in your counseling space. Create a warm and welcoming environment that reflects your brand and makes clients feel comfortable and at ease. Pay attention to the little details, such as the decor, lighting, and music, that contribute to the overall client experience.

Lastly, never underestimate the power of word-of-mouth marketing. Deliver exceptional service to your clients, and they will become your brand ambassadors, spreading the word about your practice to their friends, family, and colleagues.

Building a professional brand takes time and effort, but the rewards are well worth it. By establishing a strong brand, you will differentiate yourself from the competition, attract your ideal clients, and ultimately build a successful private counseling practice.

Creating a Compelling Website

In today's digital age, having a compelling website is essential for any business, including private counselling practices. A well-designed and informative website can act as a powerful tool to attract potential clients, establish credibility, and showcase your services. In this subchapter, we will explore the key elements of creating a compelling website for trainee counsellors looking to build their private practice.

1. Define Your Brand: Before diving into website design, it is crucial to define your brand identity. Consider your target audience, your unique selling points, and the values that guide your counselling practice. Your website should reflect your brand's personality and communicate a clear message to your potential clients.

2. Clear Navigation: A user-friendly website with clear navigation is essential for a positive user experience. Trainee counsellors should aim for a simple and intuitive menu structure, allowing visitors to easily find the information they

are looking for. Consider creating separate pages for services, about you, contact information, and blog (if applicable).

3. Engaging Content: Your website's content should be informative, engaging, and relevant to your target audience. Use clear and concise language to explain your services, approach, and areas of expertise. Consider including testimonials from past clients to build trust and credibility.

4. Professional Design: A visually appealing website that reflects professionalism is crucial for trainee counsellors looking to build trust with potential clients. Choose a clean and modern design that aligns with your brand's identity. Use high-quality images and fonts that are easy to read. Ensure that your website is mobile-responsive, as many users access the internet through their smartphones.

5. Call-to-Action: Your website should include a clear call-to-action that encourages visitors to take the next step. This could be a "Contact Me" button, a form to request more information, or a link to schedule an appointment. Make it easy for potential clients to get in touch with you.

6. Search Engine Optimization (SEO): Implement basic SEO strategies to improve your website's visibility on search engines. Research and utilize relevant keywords in your website's content, meta tags, and headings. Consider creating a blog to regularly publish informative articles that can attract organic traffic.

Creating a compelling website is an essential step for trainee counsellors looking to build a successful private practice. By clearly defining your brand, designing a user-friendly interface, and providing engaging content, you can create a website that attracts potential clients and establishes your credibility in the field. Remember to regularly update and maintain your website to ensure it remains relevant and effective in the ever-changing digital landscape.

Utilizing Social Media for Marketing

In today's digital age, it is crucial for trainee counsellors to understand the power and potential of social media in marketing their private practice. Social media platforms have emerged as valuable tools for reaching a wider audience, building brand awareness, and establishing credibility. This subchapter will explore the various ways trainee counsellors can effectively leverage social media for marketing their private practice.

First and foremost, establishing a strong online presence is essential. Trainee counsellors should create professional profiles on popular social media platforms such as Facebook, Instagram, Twitter, LinkedIn, and YouTube. These profiles should reflect the unique value they offer as counsellors and provide a glimpse into their expertise, qualifications, and specialties.

Once the profiles are set up, trainee counsellors can begin building a community and engaging with their target audience. Regularly sharing informative and relatable content is key to attracting and retaining followers. This content can include blog posts, articles, videos, podcasts, or even inspirational quotes. By consistently offering valuable insights and resources, trainee counsellors can position themselves as trusted authorities in their field.

To further extend their reach, trainee counsellors should consider collaborating with other professionals or influencers in related fields. This could involve co-creating content, hosting joint webinars or workshops, or guest appearing on each other's social media channels. Collaborations not only expose trainee counsellors to a wider audience but also provide an opportunity to exchange knowledge and gain insights from industry experts.

Another effective strategy is to encourage client testimonials and reviews. Satisfied clients can play a pivotal role in building credibility and attracting new clients. Trainee counsellors can request clients to share their positive experiences on social media platforms or provide written reviews that can be shared on their profiles or websites. Testimonials act as powerful social proof and can significantly impact the decision-making process of potential clients.

Lastly, trainee counsellors must actively engage with their audience by responding to comments, messages, and inquiries promptly. This demonstrates a genuine interest in client needs and fosters a sense of trust and connection. By engaging with their audience, trainee counsellors can also gather valuable feedback and gain insights into the specific challenges and concerns faced by their target audience.

In conclusion, social media has revolutionized the way businesses, including private counselling practices, market themselves. Trainee counsellors must harness the power of social media platforms to build their brand, connect with their audience, and ultimately grow their private practice. By utilizing these strategies, trainee counsellors can effectively utilize social media to establish themselves as successful entrepreneurs in the field of counselling.

Networking and Building Referral Relationships

In the competitive world of private counselling practice, building a strong professional network and establishing referral relationships can play a crucial role in your success as a trainee counsellor turned entrepreneur. This subchapter will guide you through the essential steps of networking and building referral relationships, empowering you to establish a thriving private practice.

1. Understanding the Importance of Networking:
Networking is not just about exchanging business cards or attending events; it is about building genuine connections with other professionals in the industry. By networking, you can expand your circle of influence, gain valuable insights, and create mutually beneficial relationships with potential referral sources.

2. Identifying Potential Referral Sources:
To build referral relationships, start by identifying potential sources within your niche. Reach out to local psychologists, psychiatrists, general

practitioners, and social workers who may encounter clients in need of counselling services. Additionally, consider connecting with complementary professionals like yoga instructors, nutritionists, or life coaches who share your target audience.

3. Building Authentic Connections:
When networking, focus on building authentic connections rather than solely promoting your services. Take the time to understand the needs and challenges of other professionals, and find ways to support them. Engage in active listening, ask meaningful questions, and offer assistance when appropriate. Building trust and rapport will increase the likelihood of receiving quality referrals.

4. Offering Value and Expertise:
Position yourself as a knowledgeable and reliable counsellor by offering value to your network. Share helpful articles, organize workshops, or give presentations on relevant topics. By showcasing your expertise, you will become the go-to person in your field, making others more likely to refer clients your way.

5. Maintaining and Nurturing Relationships:
Building referral relationships requires ongoing effort and nurturing. Stay in touch with your network by sending periodic updates, inviting them to events or workshops, or simply checking in to see how they are doing. By maintaining these connections, you ensure that your name remains at the forefront of their minds when they encounter someone in need of counselling services.

Networking and building referral relationships can be a game-changer for trainee counsellors venturing into private practice. By following the strategies outlined in this subchapter, you will lay a solid foundation for a successful and prosperous career as an entrepreneur in the counselling field. Remember, building relationships takes time, but the rewards are well worth the effort.

Implementing Advertising Strategies

As a trainee counsellor, one of your ultimate goals is to establish and run a successful private counselling practice. However, achieving this requires more than just honing your counselling skills. It also entails effectively marketing and advertising your services to reach potential clients. In this subchapter, we will delve into the essential steps and strategies for implementing successful advertising campaigns for your private practice.

The first step in implementing advertising strategies is to define your target audience. Identifying the specific group of individuals you want to cater to will enable you to tailor your advertising efforts to their needs and preferences. Consider factors such as age, gender, location, and the specific issues they may be seeking counselling for. This clarity will guide your subsequent advertising decisions.

Next, you need to establish your unique selling proposition (USP). What sets you apart from other counsellors? Perhaps you specialize in a specific therapy approach or have experience in a particular niche. Highlighting your USP in your advertising will help potential clients understand why they should choose you over your competitors.

Once you have defined your target audience and USP, it's time to choose the most effective advertising channels to reach your potential clients. Consider both online and offline options, such as social media platforms, websites, local directories, and networking events. Remember to align your advertising efforts with your audience's preferences. For example, if your target audience consists primarily of young adults, investing in social media advertising may yield better results than traditional print media.

Creating compelling and engaging advertising content is crucial to capturing your audience's attention. Craft a clear and concise message that highlights the benefits of your counselling services. Use language that resonates with your target audience and evokes emotions. Incorporate testimonials from satisfied clients to build trust and credibility.

Tracking and evaluating the effectiveness of your advertising efforts is essential for making informed decisions and refining your strategies. Use tools like Google Analytics to measure website traffic and conversion rates. Monitor the performance of your social media ads and track the number of inquiries or bookings generated through each advertising channel. This data will help you identify what is working and what needs adjustment.

Implementing advertising strategies is a continuous process. Regularly review and update your marketing efforts to stay relevant and adapt to changing market trends. By consistently refining your advertising strategies, you will increase your visibility, attract more clients, and ultimately build a thriving private counselling practice.

Chapter 7: Client Acquisition and Retention

Developing Effective Intake and Assessment Processes

As a trainee counsellor, the prospect of running your own private practice can be both exciting and daunting. One of the key aspects to consider when starting your practice is developing effective intake and assessment processes. This subchapter will guide you through the necessary steps to ensure a smooth and efficient process for welcoming clients into your practice.

The intake process is the first point of contact between you and your potential clients. It is crucial to make a positive first impression and establish a foundation of trust. Begin by creating a comprehensive intake form that captures essential client information, such as personal details, presenting issues, and previous counselling experiences. This form will serve as a starting point for your assessment process and will help you gather relevant information to inform your treatment plan.

Once you have received the completed intake form, it is time to conduct an assessment. This process involves gathering additional information about the client's concerns, goals, and expectations. Use various assessment techniques, such as open-ended questions, active listening, and observation, to gain a holistic understanding of your client's needs. This will enable you to tailor your counselling approach accordingly.

During the assessment, it is essential to establish clear boundaries and expectations. Clearly communicate your counselling approach, session fees, cancellation policies, and any other relevant information. This will ensure transparency and foster a collaborative therapeutic relationship from the outset.

Additionally, consider the ethical and legal implications of your intake and assessment processes. Familiarize yourself with the laws and regulations governing the counselling profession in your jurisdiction. Ensure that your intake process adheres to confidentiality and data protection guidelines to protect your clients' privacy and build trust.

Remember, the intake and assessment processes are not only about gathering information but also about building rapport and establishing a therapeutic alliance with your clients. Show empathy, active listening, and genuine interest in their well-being. Make sure to answer any questions or concerns they may have, as this will help them feel comfortable and confident in choosing you as their counsellor.

By developing effective intake and assessment processes, you will lay a solid foundation for your private practice. This subchapter has provided you with the necessary insights and guidelines to ensure a smooth and efficient process for welcoming clients into your practice. Embrace these practices, and you will be well on your way to building a successful counselling practice.

Designing Treatment Plans

As a trainee counsellor, one of the essential skills you need to develop is the ability to design effective treatment plans for your clients. In this subchapter, we will explore the key elements involved in creating comprehensive and client-centered treatment plans that will lay the foundation for your successful private counselling practice.

1. Assessing Client Needs:
Before designing a treatment plan, it is crucial to conduct a thorough assessment of your client's needs. This involves gathering information about their presenting issues, personal history, strengths, and resources. By understanding the client's unique circumstances, you can tailor the treatment plan to address their specific concerns effectively.

2. Setting Measurable Goals:

Treatment plans should include clear and measurable goals that both you and your client can work towards. Collaborate with your client to identify their desired outcomes and break them down into smaller, achievable objectives. Setting measurable goals allows you to track progress, evaluate the effectiveness of your interventions, and provide meaningful feedback to your client.

3. Choosing Appropriate Interventions:

Once you have identified the goals, it's time to select interventions that align with your client's needs and preferences. Different therapeutic approaches and techniques can be employed, such as cognitive-behavioral therapy, solution-focused therapy, or mindfulness-based interventions. Tailor your interventions to match your client's personality, values, and therapeutic goals, while also considering evidence-based practices.

4. Monitoring and Adjusting:

A treatment plan is a dynamic document that needs regular monitoring and adjustment. Continuously evaluate your client's progress and adapt your interventions accordingly. Encourage open communication with your clients, seeking their feedback and assessing their satisfaction with the treatment. This allows you to modify the plan as needed and ensure that it remains relevant and beneficial.

5. Collaborating with Other Professionals:

Recognize the importance of collaborating with other professionals when necessary. Referrals to specialists, such as psychiatrists, psychologists, or social workers, may be required to address specific aspects of your client's needs. Establish a network of trusted professionals to ensure your clients receive comprehensive care.

By implementing these steps, you will be able to design treatment plans that are client-centered, evidence-based, and effective. Remember that each client is unique, and their treatment plan should reflect their individual needs and goals. Developing this skill will not only enhance your effectiveness as a counsellor but also contribute to building a successful private practice.

Implementing Evidence-Based Therapeutic Techniques

As trainee counsellors embark on their journey towards building a private counselling practice, it is crucial to understand the importance of implementing evidence-based therapeutic techniques. This subchapter aims to guide trainee counsellors in effectively incorporating evidence-based practices into their private practice, ensuring the highest quality of care for their clients.

Evidence-based therapeutic techniques are interventions that have been scientifically studied and proven to be effective in treating specific mental health conditions or issues. These techniques are grounded in research and provide a solid foundation for delivering successful outcomes. By incorporating evidence-based practices into their therapeutic approach, trainee counsellors can enhance their credibility, increase client satisfaction, and achieve better client outcomes.

To begin implementing evidence-based therapeutic techniques, trainee counsellors must first familiarize themselves with the existing body of research. This includes staying up to date with the latest studies, publications, and clinical guidelines related to their area of specialization. By regularly reviewing and critically evaluating the available evidence, trainee counsellors can ensure that they are providing the most effective and appropriate interventions for their clients.

Additionally, trainee counsellors should consider attending workshops, conferences, and continuing education courses that focus on evidence-based practices. These events provide opportunities to learn from experts in the field, gain practical skills, and network with other professionals. By staying connected to the broader counselling community, trainee counsellors can access ongoing support, resources, and knowledge to enhance their practice.

Incorporating evidence-based therapeutic techniques also requires a commitment to ongoing evaluation and self-reflection. Trainee counsellors should regularly assess the effectiveness of their interventions and be open to adapting their approach based on client feedback and research findings. This continuous improvement mindset ensures that trainee counsellors are providing the most relevant and evidence-based care to their clients.

Lastly, trainee counsellors should communicate their commitment to evidence-based practices to potential clients. This can be achieved through a transparent and informative website, where trainee counsellors can showcase their knowledge, expertise, and dedication to evidence-based care. Clearly articulating the benefits of evidence-based practices can help attract clients who value and prioritize evidence-based interventions.

In conclusion, implementing evidence-based therapeutic techniques is essential for trainee counsellors looking to build a successful private counselling practice. By staying informed, attending professional development events, reflecting on their practice, and effectively communicating their commitment to evidence-based care, trainee counsellors can ensure that they are providing the highest quality of care to their clients.

Evaluating Client Progress and Outcomes

As a trainee counsellor embarking on the journey of building a private counselling practice, it is essential to understand the significance of evaluating client progress and outcomes. This subchapter aims to provide you with valuable insights and practical tools to effectively assess the efficacy of your counselling interventions.

Evaluation is a crucial aspect of any counselling practice as it enables you to measure the impact of your therapeutic interventions and ensure that your clients are receiving the support they need. By regularly evaluating client progress and outcomes, you can identify areas of improvement, modify your approaches if necessary, and enhance the overall quality of your services.

One of the primary methods of evaluating client progress is through the use of outcome measures. These standardized tools, such as questionnaires or rating scales, allow you to gather quantitative data on clients' symptoms, well-being, and overall progress. By administering these measures at regular intervals throughout the therapeutic process, you can track changes and objectively assess the effectiveness of your interventions.

Additionally, qualitative evaluation methods, such as client feedback and self-reporting, offer valuable insights into clients' subjective experiences and perceptions of their progress. Encouraging open communication and actively seeking feedback from clients can provide you with a deeper understanding of their needs and help tailor your counselling approach accordingly.

Furthermore, it is essential to consider the ethical implications and limitations of evaluating client progress. Respecting clients' autonomy and confidentiality is paramount, and their informed consent should be obtained before any evaluation takes place. It is important to explain the purpose and benefits of evaluation to clients, ensuring they feel comfortable and involved in the process.

Lastly, evaluating your own skills and professional growth as a counsellor is equally important. Engaging in regular supervision and reflective practice allows you to assess your own effectiveness, identify areas for development, and enhance your therapeutic skills. Seeking feedback from experienced colleagues and engaging in ongoing professional development activities can significantly contribute to your growth as a private practitioner.

In conclusion, evaluating client progress and outcomes is a vital component of running a successful private counselling practice. By implementing outcome measures, encouraging client feedback, and engaging in reflective practice, you can continuously improve your interventions, enhance client satisfaction, and build a reputable practice. Always remember that evaluating client progress is a collaborative process, and by actively involving your clients, you can ensure that their needs are met, and their therapeutic goals are achieved.

Building Long-Term Client Relationships

In the world of counselling, building long-term client relationships is essential for the success and growth of a private practice. As a trainee counsellor, it is crucial to understand the importance of fostering strong connections with clients to not only provide effective therapy but also to build a thriving business.

One of the fundamental aspects of building long-term client relationships is establishing a solid foundation of trust and rapport. Clients need to feel comfortable and safe in your presence to open up and share their deepest thoughts and emotions. As a trainee counsellor, focus on active listening, empathy, and non-judgmental attitude to create a supportive environment for your clients.

Consistency and reliability are key factors in building trust with your clients. Be punctual for sessions, meet deadlines, and follow through on commitments. This demonstrates your professionalism and dedication, making clients feel valued and respected. Additionally, maintaining clear and open communication channels allows clients to reach out to you whenever they need support or have questions.

Another crucial aspect of building long-term client relationships is personalized care. Every client is unique, and tailoring your approach to meet their individual needs is vital. Continually assess and adapt your therapeutic techniques, ensuring they align with the specific concerns and goals of each client. Regularly seek feedback from your clients to ensure their expectations are being met and that they feel heard and understood.

Offering ongoing support and resources beyond therapy sessions can also help foster long-term client relationships. Provide educational materials, recommend books or online resources, or even establish support groups where clients can connect with others facing similar challenges. Going the extra mile to support your clients outside of sessions shows your commitment to their well-being and helps to build a community around your practice.

Finally, do not underestimate the power of gratitude. Expressing genuine appreciation for your clients' trust and commitment can go a long way in building long-term relationships. Send thank-you notes or small tokens of appreciation to show your gratitude for their continued support. By nurturing a culture of appreciation, you create a positive and supportive atmosphere that encourages clients to stay engaged with your practice.

In conclusion, building long-term client relationships is crucial for the success of your private practice as a trainee counsellor. Focus on trust, consistency, personalized care, ongoing support, and gratitude to foster strong connections with your clients. By doing so, you will not only provide effective therapy but also build a thriving and fulfilling counselling practice.

Chapter 8: Managing Finances and Business Operations

Creating a Financial Plan and Budget

One of the most important aspects of running a successful private counselling practice is creating a solid financial plan and budget. As a trainee counsellor, it is crucial to understand the financial aspects of running a business to ensure its sustainability and profitability. In this subchapter, we will explore the key steps to creating a financial plan and budget specifically tailored for trainee counsellors venturing into private practice.

The first step in creating a financial plan is to assess your current financial situation. Take stock of your personal and professional expenses, including any debts or loans you may have. This will give you a clear understanding of your financial obligations and how they may impact your practice. It is essential to separate your personal and business finances to maintain transparency and accurately track your practice's financial health.

Next, establish your financial goals and objectives. What do you hope to achieve with your private practice? Are you looking to cover your expenses, generate a specific income, or save for future growth? Clearly defining your financial goals will guide your budgeting decisions and help you stay focused on the big picture.

Once you have established your goals, develop a budget that aligns with your practice's needs and objectives. Start by identifying your fixed expenses, such as rent, insurance, and utilities. Then, calculate your variable expenses, such as marketing and advertising costs, office supplies, and professional development. By accurately estimating these costs, you can determine your break-even point and set realistic pricing for your counselling services.

As a trainee counsellor, it is also essential to plan for any unexpected expenses or emergencies. Consider setting aside a portion of your income for an emergency fund or business savings. This will provide a safety net and ensure you can handle unforeseen circumstances without compromising the continuity of your practice.

Lastly, regularly review and adjust your financial plan and budget as needed. As your practice grows and evolves, your financial needs may change. Stay proactive and regularly evaluate your progress towards your goals, making any necessary adjustments to your budget along the way.

In conclusion, creating a financial plan and budget is a vital step for trainee counsellors looking to run a successful private practice. By assessing your current financial situation, setting clear goals, developing a comprehensive budget, planning for unexpected expenses, and regularly reviewing your progress, you will be well-equipped to navigate the financial challenges of entrepreneurship and ensure the long-term success of your counselling practice.

Tracking Income and Expenses

As a trainee counsellor, one of your goals may be to eventually run your own private practice. While this can be an exciting and rewarding venture, it also comes with its fair share of responsibilities, especially when it comes to managing your finances. Tracking your income and expenses is crucial for the success of your private counselling practice, and in this subchapter, we will explore the importance of this task and provide you with some practical tips to get started.

Why is tracking income and expenses important? Well, for starters, it allows you to have a clear picture of your financial health. By keeping track of every penny that comes in and goes out, you can monitor your practice's profitability and identify areas where you may need to make adjustments. This knowledge will help you make informed decisions about pricing, budgeting, and even hiring additional support staff as your practice grows.

To effectively track your income, start by creating a system that suits your needs. This could be as simple as using a spreadsheet or investing in accounting software specifically designed for small businesses. Whichever method you choose, it's essential to record every payment received accurately, including the date, client name, and amount. Categorizing your income sources can also be helpful, as it allows you to identify which services or clients bring in the most revenue.

On the expense side, it's essential to keep track of your business-related costs. This includes expenses such as rent, utilities, office supplies, marketing, and professional development. By monitoring your expenses, you can identify areas where you may be overspending or find opportunities to cut costs. This knowledge will help you create a realistic budget and ensure that you are maximizing your practice's profitability.

In addition to tracking income and expenses, it's also crucial to set aside funds for taxes. As a private practice owner, you will be responsible for paying your own taxes, including income tax and possibly self-employment tax. By setting aside a portion of your income regularly, you can avoid any surprises come tax season and ensure that you are compliant with the law.

In conclusion, tracking your income and expenses is an essential aspect of running a successful private counselling practice. It provides you with a clear picture of your financial health, helps you make informed decisions, and ensures that you are maximizing your profitability. By implementing a system and regularly monitoring your finances, you will be well on your way to becoming a successful entrepreneur in the counselling field.

Understanding Billing Processes

In the journey from being a trainee counsellor to becoming an entrepreneur with your private counselling practice, it is crucial to have a solid understanding of billing processes. As a trainee counsellor, you may have limited exposure to the intricacies of billing, but it is an essential aspect of running a successful private practice. This subchapter aims to provide you with a comprehensive understanding of billing processes and their significance in your practice.

1. The Importance of Accurate Billing:
Accurate billing is the foundation of a successful private counselling practice. It enables you to maintain financial stability, track client sessions, and ensure fairness in your fees. Understanding how to create and manage invoices, track payment due dates, and handle insurance claims will contribute to the professionalism and efficiency of your practice.

2. Creating Invoices:
Creating clear and concise invoices is crucial for both you and your clients. Learn how to include essential details such as session dates, duration, fees, and payment methods on your invoices. This will help you maintain an organized record of your clients' sessions and facilitate transparent communication about payment expectations.

3. Setting Fees:
Determining appropriate fees for your counselling services is a crucial aspect of billing processes. Explore different pricing models and industry standards to ensure your fees are competitive and reflect the value you provide. You may also want to consider offering sliding scale fees or other payment options to accommodate clients with different financial capacities.

4. Insurance Claims:
Understanding how insurance claims work is essential if you plan to work with clients who have insurance coverage. Familiarize yourself with the process of submitting claims, including the required documentation and any specific guidelines from insurance providers. This knowledge will save you time and effort when dealing with insurance companies.

5. Record-Keeping and Bookkeeping:
Maintaining accurate records of your billing activities is vital for the financial health of your practice. Explore bookkeeping systems and software that can

help you track your income, expenses, and tax obligations. This will not only make your billing processes more efficient but also ensure compliance with legal and regulatory requirements.

6. Handling Late Payments and Non-Payments:
Despite your best efforts, there may be instances where clients fail to make timely payments or do not pay at all. Learn how to handle these situations professionally and assertively. Establish clear policies regarding late payments and non-payments, and communicate them to your clients. This will help you navigate potentially uncomfortable conversations while safeguarding your practice's financial stability.

By understanding billing processes thoroughly, you will be better equipped to manage the financial aspects of your private counselling practice. Remember that billing is not just about money; it is about maintaining professionalism, building trust with your clients, and ensuring the sustainability of your practice.

Managing Cash Flow and Taxes

As a trainee counsellor, embarking on the journey of running a private practice can be both exciting and overwhelming. One crucial aspect that you need to master is managing your cash flow and taxes. Understanding and effectively handling these financial aspects will not only ensure the smooth operation of your practice but also pave the way for your success as an entrepreneur.

Cash flow management is about monitoring and controlling the movement of money in and out of your practice. It is essential to maintain a healthy cash flow to meet your financial obligations, such as rent, utilities, and personal expenses, while also investing in the growth and development of your practice.

To effectively manage your cash flow, start by creating a budget that outlines your expected income and expenses. This will help you identify any potential cash shortfalls or surplus. Consider setting aside a portion of your income for contingencies and unexpected expenses.

Implementing a system for tracking your income and expenses is another crucial aspect of cash flow management. Utilize accounting software or hire a bookkeeper to keep your financial records organized. Regularly review your financial statements, such as profit and loss statements and balance sheets, to gain insights into the financial health of your practice.

Understanding and complying with tax obligations is equally vital for running a successful private practice. Familiarize yourself with the tax laws and regulations specific to your country or region. Maintain accurate records of your income and expenses to ensure accurate tax reporting.

Consider consulting with a tax professional who specializes in small businesses or sole proprietorships. They can guide you through the complexities of tax planning, deductions, and filing requirements. Taking advantage of available tax deductions and credits can significantly reduce your tax liability and help you keep more of your hard-earned income.

In addition to managing cash flow and taxes, it is also essential to cultivate a mindset of financial responsibility. Practice disciplined spending, save for the future, and invest in your professional development. Building a solid financial foundation will not only benefit your practice but also your personal and professional growth.

By mastering the art of managing cash flow and taxes, you will be well on your way to building a thriving private counselling practice. Remember, financial management is an ongoing process that requires continuous monitoring and adjustment. Stay proactive, seek professional advice when needed, and never underestimate the power of sound financial practices in achieving your entrepreneurial goals.

Streamlining Business Operations

In the journey from being a trainee counsellor to becoming a successful entrepreneur, it is crucial to understand the importance of streamlining your business operations. Efficiently managing your private counselling practice not only ensures smooth day-to-day operations but also contributes to the overall growth and success of your business. In this subchapter, we will explore key strategies and techniques to streamline your business operations effectively.

One of the first steps towards streamlining your private practice is to establish clear and well-defined processes and procedures. This includes creating a structured system for client intake, appointment scheduling, and record-keeping. By implementing standardized procedures, trainee counsellors can ensure that each step of their practice is conducted consistently, minimizing errors and improving efficiency.

Another essential aspect of streamlining business operations is adopting technology and automation. Embracing digital tools, such as appointment scheduling software, billing systems, and electronic record-keeping, can significantly streamline administrative tasks. Automating these processes not only saves time but also reduces the risk of human error and enhances the overall client experience.

Additionally, trainee counsellors should prioritize effective communication and collaboration within their practice. Establishing clear channels of communication with clients, colleagues, and other professionals in the field is vital. Utilizing technology such as video conferencing for remote sessions or virtual team meetings can help streamline communication and enhance collaboration, especially in today's digital age.

Moreover, trainee counsellors should consider outsourcing certain non-core functions of their practice to professional service providers. This could include tasks such as accounting, marketing, or IT support. By delegating these responsibilities to experts, trainee counsellors can focus on their core competencies and dedicate more time to providing quality counselling services to their clients.

Lastly, continuous evaluation and improvement are essential for streamlining business operations. Regularly reviewing your processes, seeking feedback from clients and colleagues, and identifying areas of improvement are crucial steps in enhancing efficiency and refining your practice over time.

In conclusion, streamlining business operations is a fundamental aspect of running a successful private counselling practice. By establishing clear processes, leveraging technology, fostering effective communication, outsourcing non-core tasks, and continuously improving, trainee counsellors can achieve optimal efficiency and provide exceptional services to their clients. Embracing these strategies will not only enhance the overall experience for both counsellors and clients but also contribute to the long-term success and growth of the private practice.

Business and Public Liability Insurance

As a trainee counsellor venturing into the world of running a private practice, it is essential to understand the importance of business and public liability insurance. This subchapter aims to provide you with a comprehensive overview of these insurances and their significance in safeguarding your practice.

Business liability insurance, also known as professional indemnity insurance, protects you against claims made by clients who may feel dissatisfied with your services. It covers legal fees, settlements, and other related costs in case a client sues you for negligence or professional misconduct. This insurance is crucial for counsellors as it provides financial protection and ensures that you can continue practicing without the fear of financial ruin.

Public liability insurance, on the other hand, covers you in case someone is injured or their property is damaged as a result of your business activities. For instance, if a client slips and falls in your office, this insurance will help cover any medical expenses or legal costs that may arise from the incident. Public liability insurance is essential for any business, including private counselling practices, as it offers protection against unforeseen accidents or mishaps.

By investing in business and public liability insurance, you are not only protecting your practice but also demonstrating professionalism and trustworthiness to your clients. Insurance coverage reassures clients that you are committed to their well-being and are prepared to handle any potential issues that may arise during the counselling process.

When choosing insurance providers, it is crucial to consider factors such as coverage limits, premiums, and the specific needs of your practice. Conduct thorough research and consult with insurance professionals to ensure you select the most suitable policies for your private counselling practice.

Furthermore, it is essential to regularly review and update your insurance coverage as your practice grows and evolves. As you acquire more clients and expand your services, your insurance needs may change. It is recommended to review your policies annually to ensure that you have adequate coverage to protect your practice against potential risks.

In conclusion, business and public liability insurance are essential components of running a private counselling practice. These insurances provide financial protection, demonstrate professionalism, and offer peace of mind to both you and your clients. By investing in comprehensive coverage and regularly reviewing your policies, you can safeguard your practice and focus on providing high-quality counselling services to your clients.

Chapter 9: Self-Care and Professional Development

Prioritizing Self-Care as a Counsellor

As a trainee counsellor, it is crucial to understand the significance of prioritizing self-care in your journey towards building a successful private practice. The demands of the counselling profession can be emotionally and mentally taxing, making it essential for counsellors to take care of themselves to maintain their well-being and provide effective support to their clients.

Self-care involves intentionally taking time to nurture and replenish your own physical, emotional, and mental well-being. It is not a luxury but a necessity for those in the helping profession. By prioritizing self-care, trainee counsellors can ensure they have the resilience and energy needed to navigate the challenges of running a private practice.

One aspect of self-care is setting healthy boundaries. As a trainee counsellor, it is easy to become consumed by the needs of clients and neglect your own needs. Learning to set limits on your availability and creating a work-life balance is crucial for avoiding burnout and maintaining your own mental health.

Another important aspect is establishing a self-care routine. This can include engaging in activities that promote relaxation and well-being such as exercise, meditation, journaling, or spending time in nature. By incorporating these practices into your daily or weekly schedule, you can create a self-care routine that works for you.

Additionally, seeking supervision and support from fellow trainee counsellors or experienced professionals is vital. Regular supervision sessions can provide a safe space to reflect on your work, discuss any challenges, and receive guidance. Surrounding yourself with a supportive network of colleagues who understand the unique demands of the counselling profession can also be invaluable.

Remember, self-care is not selfish; it is an investment in your own well-being and the quality of care you can provide to your clients. By prioritizing self-care, you are better equipped to manage stress, maintain a healthy work-life balance, and sustain your passion for counselling.

In conclusion, as a trainee counsellor, it is crucial to prioritize self-care in order to build a successful private practice. By setting healthy boundaries, establishing a self-care routine, seeking supervision and support, trainee counsellors can ensure their own well-being while providing effective support to their clients. Remember, self-care is not a luxury; it is a necessity for those in the counselling profession.

Managing Stress and Burnout

As a trainee counsellor, embarking on the journey of building your own private practice can be both exciting and overwhelming. While it offers immense professional growth and the opportunity to make a positive impact on people's lives, it also comes with its fair share of challenges. One of the most important aspects of running a successful private counselling practice is managing stress and preventing burnout.

Stress is an inevitable part of any profession, but it can be particularly overwhelming in the field of counselling. Dealing with clients' emotional struggles and personal challenges on a daily basis can take a toll on your own well-being. Therefore, it is crucial to implement effective strategies to manage stress and prevent burnout.

First and foremost, self-care should be your top priority. Take care of your physical, emotional, and mental health by engaging in activities that bring you joy and relaxation. Set aside time for exercise, hobbies, and spending quality time with loved ones. Remember, you cannot pour from an empty cup, so ensure you are nurturing yourself.

It is also important to establish healthy boundaries with your clients. While it is natural to empathize with their struggles, it is essential to maintain a professional distance to protect your own emotional well-being. Learn to recognize your limits and refer clients to other professionals when necessary. Remember, you are not responsible for fixing or solving all of their problems.

Seeking support from peers and supervisors is another valuable resource for managing stress. Join professional counseling associations or networking groups to connect with fellow trainee counsellors who are going through similar experiences. Sharing your challenges and learning from others can provide a sense of camaraderie and support.

Additionally, regular supervision sessions can be immensely helpful in preventing burnout. Supervision allows you to discuss your cases, explore any countertransference issues, and receive guidance from experienced professionals. It provides a safe space to reflect on your practice and address any challenges or concerns that may be contributing to stress.

Lastly, remember to set realistic expectations for yourself. Building a private practice takes time and effort, and it is normal to encounter setbacks along the way. Be patient with yourself and celebrate small victories. Recognize that stress is a part of the growth process and use it as an opportunity to learn and develop resilience.

In conclusion, managing stress and preventing burnout is essential for trainee counsellors embarking on the journey of building their own private practice. By prioritizing self-care, setting healthy boundaries, seeking support, and maintaining realistic expectations, you can create a sustainable and fulfilling career in private counselling. Remember, your well-being is just as important as that of your clients.

Seeking Supervision and Peer Support

In the world of counseling, the journey from being a trainee to becoming an entrepreneur and running a private practice can be both exciting and daunting. As a trainee counselor, it is crucial to recognize the importance of seeking supervision and peer support throughout this transition. This subchapter will guide you through the benefits of supervision and the significance of peer support in building a successful private counseling practice.

Supervision is a vital aspect of professional growth and development for trainee counselors. It provides a safe and supportive environment where you can reflect on your practice, gain valuable insights, and receive guidance from an experienced supervisor. Supervision offers a space to discuss challenging cases, ethical dilemmas, and personal struggles that may arise while working with clients. It helps you develop self-awareness, enhance your skills, and maintain ethical standards in your practice. By seeking supervision, you demonstrate a commitment to ongoing learning and improvement, which is essential for building a reputable private counseling practice.

Peer support is equally important in your journey from being a trainee to an entrepreneur. Connecting with fellow trainee counselors can provide a source of encouragement, empathy, and shared experiences. Peer support allows you to discuss common challenges, exchange ideas, and learn from each other's successes and failures. Through peer networks, you can access a wealth of knowledge and resources, expand your professional network, and even collaborate on joint projects. Additionally, peer support can contribute to your overall well-being by reducing feelings of isolation and providing a sense of belonging within the counseling community.

When seeking supervision and peer support, it is essential to choose the right individuals or groups. Look for supervisors who are experienced, knowledgeable, and aligned with your professional values. Seek out peer support networks that focus on your specific niche within counseling or private practice. Online forums, professional associations, and local counseling groups can be valuable resources for finding suitable supervisors and connecting with peers.

In conclusion, seeking supervision and peer support is a fundamental step in the journey from trainee to entrepreneur. These support systems provide invaluable guidance, insight, and emotional support as you navigate the challenges and opportunities of running a private counseling practice. Embrace the opportunities for self-reflection, professional growth, and connection that supervision and peer support offer, as they will help you develop the skills and confidence needed to thrive in the counseling profession.

Continuing Education and Skill Enhancement

In the ever-evolving field of counseling, it is crucial for trainee counselors to recognize the importance of continuing education and skill enhancement. As you embark on your journey from trainee to entrepreneur, building a private counseling practice, investing in your professional development becomes paramount. This subchapter aims to guide you in understanding the significance of continuous learning and provide you with practical strategies to enhance your skills.

As a trainee counselor, your education and training are just the beginning of your professional growth. Continuing education allows you to stay updated with the latest research, theories, and techniques in the field. By pursuing advanced courses, attending workshops, or participating in conferences, you open doors to new knowledge and perspectives, ensuring that you provide the best possible care for your clients.

Moreover, continuing education helps you specialize in specific areas of counseling, enabling you to cater to the unique needs of your target audience. Whether it is trauma-informed therapy, couples counseling, or child psychology, expanding your expertise through ongoing learning will set you apart from other practitioners and increase your chances of success in your private practice.

Skill enhancement is equally crucial in building a thriving counseling practice. Beyond theoretical knowledge, it is essential to develop and refine your practical skills. This includes honing your communication, active listening, and empathy skills, as well as learning effective techniques for building rapport with clients. Additionally, developing skills in areas such as assessment, treatment planning, and outcome measurement will enhance your ability to provide evidence-based and client-centered care.

To enhance your skills, seek opportunities for supervision and mentoring from experienced practitioners. Engage in peer consultations and case discussions to gain insights and perspectives from fellow trainees and established professionals. Embrace the power of self-reflection and self-assessment, identifying areas for improvement and setting goals for your skill development.

Remember, continuing education and skill enhancement are ongoing processes throughout your career as a counselor. It is not a one-time endeavor but a lifelong commitment to excellence in your practice. By investing in your professional development, you not only benefit yourself but also ensure the best possible outcomes for your clients.

In conclusion, as you transition from a trainee to entrepreneur, never underestimate the power of continuing education and skill enhancement. Embrace the opportunities to expand your knowledge, specialize in specific areas, and enhance your practical skills. By doing so, you will establish yourself as a competent and compassionate counselor, ready to run a successful private practice and make a positive impact in the lives of your clients.

Nurturing Personal and Professional Growth

As trainee counsellors, the journey towards building a private counselling practice can be both exciting and challenging. Along the way, it is crucial to recognize and prioritize the importance of nurturing personal and professional growth. This subchapter delves into the various aspects of personal and professional development, providing valuable insights and guidance to help you thrive in your journey from trainee to entrepreneur.

Personal growth forms the foundation of your professional growth. It involves self-awareness, self-reflection, and self-care. Taking the time to understand your strengths, weaknesses, values, and beliefs is essential in shaping your therapeutic approach and establishing your unique counseling style. Engaging in personal therapy or supervision can offer valuable opportunities for self-reflection, helping you gain insights into yourself and your interactions with clients.

Additionally, self-care plays a significant role in your personal growth. As you embark on the challenging path of building a private practice, it is crucial to prioritize self-care to prevent burnout and maintain your overall well-being. Self-care can include activities like exercise, meditation, spending time in nature, cultivating hobbies, and connecting with loved ones. Remember, taking care of yourself is not a luxury but a necessity, as it directly impacts your ability to provide quality care to your clients.

Professional growth, on the other hand, focuses on developing the skills and knowledge necessary for running a successful private practice. This includes staying up-to-date with the latest research and therapeutic techniques, attending relevant workshops and conferences, and engaging in ongoing professional development opportunities. Building a network of fellow counsellors and mentors can provide invaluable support and guidance throughout your journey.

Furthermore, developing a business mindset is crucial for the success of your private practice. This involves understanding the basics of marketing, branding, and financial management. Learning how to effectively market your services, create a strong brand identity, and manage your finances can significantly contribute to the growth and sustainability of your practice.

In conclusion, nurturing personal and professional growth is essential for trainee counsellors aspiring to build a private practice. By investing in self-awareness, self-care, and ongoing professional development, you can establish a solid foundation for your counseling career. Remember, personal and professional growth is a lifelong journey, and embracing it will not only benefit you but also the clients you serve.

Chapter 10: Overcoming Challenges and Embracing Success

Identifying Common Challenges in Private Practice

Starting a private counselling practice can be an exciting and rewarding step in your career as a trainee counsellor. However, it is essential to recognize and prepare for the common challenges that may arise along the way. In this subchapter, we will explore some of the most prevalent obstacles faced by trainee counsellors when running a private practice.

One of the primary challenges many trainee counsellors encounter is building a consistent and reliable client base. Establishing a solid referral network and marketing your services effectively can be a daunting task. It is crucial to develop a comprehensive marketing strategy that includes online platforms, networking events, and collaborations with other professionals in the field. Building a strong online presence through a website and social media can also significantly help attract potential clients.

Another common hurdle is managing the financial aspects of a private practice. As a trainee counsellor, it is essential to set realistic and competitive fees while still ensuring financial sustainability. Developing a clear pricing structure and understanding the local market rates can help you strike the right balance between affordability and profitability.

Managing time and workload is another challenge faced by trainee counsellors. Balancing client appointments with administrative tasks, continuing professional development, and self-care can be overwhelming. Learning effective time management techniques, setting boundaries, and seeking support from mentors or supervisors can help you navigate these challenges successfully.

Maintaining ethical and legal standards is crucial in private practice. Adhering to the ethical guidelines set by professional bodies and staying up-to-date with legal requirements can be demanding. Familiarize yourself with the relevant professional codes of ethics, data protection regulations, and other legal obligations to ensure the highest standards of care and confidentiality for your clients.

Lastly, self-doubt and imposter syndrome can be significant psychological challenges when starting a private practice. Trainee counsellors may question their skills, experience, or readiness to run a business independently. It is important to recognize and address these feelings by seeking supervision or peer support, engaging in personal therapy, and continuously investing in your professional development.

By identifying and preparing for these common challenges, trainee counsellors can navigate the path from trainee to entrepreneur more confidently. Remember, building a successful private practice takes time, effort, and perseverance. With the right strategies and support, you can overcome these obstacles and create a thriving counselling practice that serves both you and your clients.

Developing Strategies for Problem Solving

When starting a private counselling practice, trainee counsellors may encounter a variety of challenges along the way. Developing effective strategies for problem-solving is essential to overcome these obstacles and build a successful practice. This subchapter will explore some key strategies that can help trainee counsellors navigate the complexities of running a private practice.

1. Identify the Problem: The first step in problem-solving is to clearly define and identify the issue at hand. Trainee counsellors should analyze and understand the problem before attempting to find a solution. This involves gathering relevant information, considering different perspectives, and determining the root cause of the problem.

2. Brainstorming Solutions: Once the problem is identified, it is important to generate a range of possible solutions. Trainee counsellors can engage in brainstorming sessions, where they can freely express ideas without judgment. Encouraging creativity and considering all options will help in developing a comprehensive list of potential solutions.

3. Evaluate and Select a Solution: After generating a list of possible solutions, trainee counsellors should evaluate each option based on its feasibility, effectiveness, and alignment with their practice's values. It is crucial to consider the potential risks and benefits associated with each solution. Ultimately, a solution should be selected that is practical, ethical, and aligns with the trainee counsellor's goals.

4. Implementation: Once a solution is chosen, it is time to put it into action. Trainee counsellors should create a plan outlining the steps needed to implement the chosen solution effectively. This may involve seeking additional resources, collaborating with others, or developing new skills. It is important to be proactive and take decisive action to address the problem.

5. Reflect and Learn: Problem-solving is an iterative process, and trainee counsellors should reflect on the outcomes of their chosen solution. By evaluating the effectiveness of the implemented solution, trainee counsellors can learn from their experiences and make adjustments if necessary. Reflection and learning are essential for personal and professional growth.

6. Seek Support: Trainee counsellors should not hesitate to seek support from mentors, supervisors, or fellow professionals when faced with challenging problems. Sharing experiences, seeking advice, and learning from others' perspectives can provide valuable insights and alternative solutions.

By developing effective strategies for problem-solving, trainee counsellors can confidently navigate the complexities of running a private practice. These strategies will enable them to tackle challenges head-on, make informed decisions, and build a successful counselling practice that positively impacts their clients' lives.

Celebrating Milestones and Achievements

As trainee counsellors, embarking on the journey of building a private counselling practice can be both exhilarating and daunting. The road to becoming a successful entrepreneur in this field is filled with challenges, but it is also sprinkled with moments of triumph and celebration. In this subchapter, we will explore the importance of acknowledging and commemorating the milestones and achievements along this path.

First and foremost, it is crucial to recognize that every step forward is a milestone in itself. From completing your training program to obtaining your license, each accomplishment is a testament to your dedication and hard work. Take the time to acknowledge these milestones and give yourself a pat on the back. Celebrating these achievements not only boosts your confidence but also serves as a reminder of how far you have come.

In addition to personal milestones, it is equally important to celebrate the achievements of your clients. As a trainee counsellor, you may experience a range of emotions when you witness the growth and progress of those you work with. Take the opportunity to celebrate these moments with your clients, as it not only validates their journey but also strengthens the therapeutic relationship. By acknowledging their achievements, you are creating a positive and empowering environment that fosters continued growth.

Furthermore, celebrating milestones and achievements can also serve as a form of motivation. As you encounter obstacles and face setbacks, reflecting on past successes can reignite your passion and remind you of your capabilities. Use these moments as fuel to propel yourself forward, knowing that each milestone achieved brings you closer to your ultimate goal of running a successful private practice.

Lastly, celebrating milestones and achievements should not be limited to individual experiences. Consider creating a supportive community of trainee counsellors who can share in your triumphs and offer valuable insights. Organize networking events or support groups where you can come together to celebrate each other's accomplishments. By doing so, you not only strengthen your professional network but also create a sense of camaraderie and shared purpose.

In conclusion, celebrating milestones and achievements is vital to the journey of building a private counselling practice as a trainee counsellor. Whether it be personal milestones, client successes, or creating a supportive community, these celebrations serve as reminders of progress, motivation during challenging times, and opportunities for connection. Embrace these moments of celebration and allow them to fuel your growth and inspire you to continue on the path towards becoming a successful entrepreneur in the field of counselling.

Embracing a Growth Mindset

In the journey from trainee to entrepreneur, one of the most crucial qualities you can develop is a growth mindset. A growth mindset is the belief that your abilities and intelligence can be developed through dedication, effort, and a willingness to learn from both successes and failures. As trainee counsellors, embracing a growth mindset is vital for navigating the challenges of running a private practice successfully.

When starting a private counselling practice, you may encounter numerous obstacles and setbacks. It is in these moments that a growth mindset becomes your greatest asset. Instead of viewing failures as permanent and insurmountable, a growth mindset allows you to see them as opportunities for growth and learning. With each setback, you can reflect on what went wrong, adapt your approach, and try again. This mindset will help you persevere through difficult times and ultimately lead to personal and professional growth.

Another aspect of a growth mindset is the willingness to seek out new knowledge and skills. As a trainee counsellor transitioning into running your own private practice, it is essential to continually educate yourself and stay updated on industry trends and best practices. Attend workshops, conferences, and seminars related to your field, and engage in ongoing professional development. By embracing a growth mindset, you open yourself up to new possibilities and expand your expertise, ultimately benefiting your clients and your practice.

Moreover, a growth mindset encourages you to embrace challenges and step out of your comfort zone. Running a private practice requires taking on various responsibilities, such as marketing, networking, and managing finances. Embracing a growth mindset means viewing these challenges as opportunities for personal and professional growth. Instead of shying away from tasks outside your comfort zone, approach them with enthusiasm and a willingness to learn. This mindset will help you develop new skills and become a more well-rounded entrepreneur.

In conclusion, embracing a growth mindset is crucial for trainee counsellors transitioning into running a private practice. By viewing setbacks as opportunities, seeking out new knowledge, and embracing challenges, you will grow both personally and professionally. Remember that the journey from trainee to entrepreneur is a continuous learning experience, and a growth mindset will be your guiding light along the way.

Sustaining and Expanding Your Private Counselling Practice

Congratulations on taking the first step towards building your private counselling practice! As a trainee counsellor, embarking on this journey can be both exciting and daunting. In this subchapter, we will explore essential strategies and insights to help you sustain and expand your private counselling practice.

Building a successful private practice requires a solid foundation. Start by defining your niche and target audience. By specializing in a specific area, such as anxiety, relationships, or trauma, you can develop a reputation as an expert in that field. This will attract clients who are seeking help in that particular area, allowing you to establish yourself as a go-to counsellor.

Networking is crucial in the counselling field, especially when starting out. Connect with other professionals in your community, such as doctors, social workers, or psychologists. Building relationships with these individuals can lead to referrals, collaborations, and a wider client base. Attend conferences, workshops, and seminars to stay updated on the latest research and connect with like-minded professionals.

Investing in marketing and branding is essential for growing your private practice. Create a professional website that showcases your services, qualifications, and testimonials from satisfied clients. Utilize social media platforms, such as Facebook or Instagram, to engage with your audience and share valuable content. Consider offering free resources, such as blog posts or downloadable guides, to establish yourself as a trusted expert in your field.

Client retention is key to sustaining your practice. Provide exceptional service by being empathetic, non-judgmental, and maintaining strict confidentiality. Regularly ask for feedback to ensure client satisfaction and identify areas for improvement. Consider offering loyalty programs or special discounts to encourage clients to continue sessions and refer others to your practice.

Expanding your private practice requires careful planning and consideration. As you gain experience and build a solid client base, you may consider hiring additional therapists or expanding your services to include group therapy or workshops. However, ensure that you have the necessary resources and infrastructure in place to support such growth.

Remember, building a private counselling practice takes time and dedication. Embrace continuous learning, seek supervision or mentorship, and stay connected to the counselling community. By implementing these strategies and maintaining a strong focus on client care, you can build a thriving private counselling practice that positively impacts the lives of many individuals.

In conclusion, "Sustaining and Expanding Your Private Counselling Practice" is a crucial subchapter that provides trainee counsellors with valuable insights and strategies to establish and grow their private practice. By defining your niche, networking, investing in marketing and branding, ensuring client satisfaction, and planning for expansion, you can build a successful and fulfilling career as a private counsellor.

Conclusion: Your Journey from Trainee to Successful Entrepreneur

Congratulations! You have reached the end of this book, "From Trainee to Entrepreneur: Building a Private Counselling Practice." Throughout this journey, we have explored the essential steps and valuable insights to help you transition from a trainee counsellor to a successful entrepreneur in the field of private counselling practice.

As a trainee counsellor, you embarked on this path with a passion for helping others and a desire to make a difference in people's lives. We have discussed the importance of honing your counselling skills, acquiring the necessary qualifications, and gaining practical experience to build a solid foundation for your future practice.

In this subchapter, we will reflect on the key lessons learned and the exciting road that lies ahead as you embark on your journey as an entrepreneur in the private counselling industry.

First and foremost, we have emphasized the significance of developing a clear and comprehensive business plan. This plan serves as a roadmap for your practice, outlining your objectives, target market, marketing strategies, and financial projections. It is crucial to set goals and regularly review and revise your plan to adapt to the ever-changing landscape of this industry.

Additionally, we have explored various marketing techniques and strategies to help you effectively promote your private counselling practice. From building a strong online presence through a professional website and social media platforms to networking with other professionals and leveraging referrals, you have learned how to position yourself as a trusted and reputable counsellor.

Furthermore, we have delved into the importance of self-care as an entrepreneur. Running a private practice can be demanding and emotionally draining, making it essential to prioritize your own well-being. We have discussed the significance of setting boundaries, seeking supervision and support, and practicing self-compassion to maintain your energy and passion for your work.

Lastly, we have touched on the continuous professional development and growth that is necessary to succeed in this field. As an entrepreneur, it is crucial to stay updated with the latest research, theories, and techniques in counselling. Engaging in ongoing training, attending workshops and conferences, and seeking supervision will not only enhance your skills but also ensure that you provide the highest quality of care to your clients.

In conclusion, your journey from trainee to successful entrepreneur in the field of private counselling practice is an exciting and rewarding one. By following the steps outlined in this book, you have laid a strong foundation for your future practice. Remember to stay focused, adapt to changes, and never stop learning and growing. Your dedication, passion, and commitment to helping others will undoubtedly make a positive impact on the lives of your clients. Good luck on your entrepreneurial journey!

www.ingramcontent.com/pod-product-compliance
Lightning Source LLC
Chambersburg PA
CBHW062355290526
45794CB00005B/2232